The Queen's Government

*

SIR IVOR JENNINGS
K.B.E., Q.C.

GREENWOOD PRESS, PUBLISHERS
WESTPORT, CONNECTICUT

Library of Congress Cataloging in Publication Data

Jennings, Ivor, Sir, 1903-1965.
  The Queen's government.

  Reprint. Originally published: Reprinted (with
revisions). Harmondsworth, Middlesex, England ; Baltimore,
Md., U.S.A. : Penguin Books, 1965 printing, c1954.
  Bibliography: p.
  Includes index.
  1. Great Britain--Politics and government--20th
century. I. Title.
JN231.J46 1984   320.941   84-12767
ISBN 0-313-24571-1 (lib. bdg.)

Reprinted with the permission of Penguin Books Ltd

Reprinted in 1984 by Greenwood Press
A division of Congressional Information Service, Inc.
88 Post Road West, Westport, Connecticut 06881

Printed in the United States of America

10 9 8 7 6 5 4 3 2 1

Contents

*

PREFACE   7

CHAPTER 1 : *Freedom under the Law*

THE RULE OF LAW   9
PARLIAMENTARY SOVEREIGNTY   13
DEMOCRACY   20
THE TYRANNY OF THE MAJORITY   27

CHAPTER 2 : *The Queen*

THE QUEEN   30
THE CROWN   30
THE QUEEN AND THE COMMONWEALTH   36
THE QUEEN IN PERSON   40
THE QUEEN AND THE COMMON MAN   46

CHAPTER 3 : *Politics*

THE IMPORTANCE OF POLITICS   50
POLITICS AND THE SOCIAL CLASSES   51
THE TWO-PARTY SYSTEM   62

CHAPTER 4 : *The Queen in Parliament*

THE QUEEN   66
THE HOUSE OF LORDS   71
THE HOUSE OF COMMONS   76

CHAPTER 5 : *Her Majesty's Government*

THE TRANSFER OF POWER   95
AGENCIES OF GOVERNMENT   101
THE CIVIL SERVICE   104
MINISTERIAL CONTROL   108

CHAPTER 6 : *Cabinet Government*

THE MINISTRY AND THE CABINET 114
COLLECTIVE RESPONSIBILITY   118
CABINET PROCEDURE   125
GOVERNMENT AND OPINION   129

CHAPTER 7 : *The Prime Minister*

THE OFFICE   132
FUNCTIONS   134

CHAPTER 8 : *The Queen's Justice*

LAW AND OPINION   141
THE INDEPENDENCE OF THE JUDICIARY 145
FUNCTIONS OF THE JUDICIARY   147
GOVERNMENT ACCORDING TO LAW 152

FURTHER READING   155

INDEX   157

Preface

*

A DESCRIPTION of the British Constitution may use one or more of four methods: the historical, the legal, the analytical, and the critical. The last requires the adoption of philosophical or political assumptions and it has generally been avoided in this book, though it will be seen that I have adopted the principles of liberalism and toleration which are implicit in the Constitution itself. All the other methods have been used in such a manner as to give the reader a general introduction to the Constitution so that he can, if he pleases, undertake further reading in any of the three fields of study. Inevitably there are some ideas common to this book and to my book on *The British Constitution* (Cambridge University Press, 4th ed., 1951), but generally the treatment is different.

The careful reader will note some repetition in different Chapters. The explanation is that the whole Constitution hangs together and that, in a book of this character, it seems better to make the same point twice in different connexions than to supply cross-references.

W. I. J.

TRINITY HALL
CAMBRIDGE
25 November 1964

*

THE RULE OF LAW

IF an Englishman (who may be regarded as typical of the peoples of the Commonwealth) were to put his fundamental political beliefs into a single formula it would go something like this:

No man (or woman) may be arrested by a policeman unless he has broken the law, nor be kept in prison unless a magistrate or a judge and jury have found him guilty of an offence; nor may he be deprived of his property except by a legal proceeding and then only on payment of compensation; nor may any Government official push him around unless the law says he may, and then only if the official strictly obeys all the legal formalities and makes certain that the man has a square deal. And if anybody breaks these rules the person concerned is fully entitled to go along and complain to a justice of the peace, or write to the papers and make a fuss or ask his Member to raise the question in Parliament.

It is an interesting formula, for in principle it is not very different from that to which King John agreed at Runnymede in 1215:

Nullus liber homo capiatur vel imprisonetur aut disseisietur aut utlagetur aut aliquo modo destruatur, nec super eum ibimus, nec super eum mittemus, nisi per legale judicum parium suorum, vel per legem terre.

The exact meaning of this famous 39th Article of Magna Carta is a matter of some controversy, but it may reasonably be translated as follows:

No free man shall be taken or imprisoned or disseised (i.e. deprived of his lands) or outlawed or in any way destroyed, nor will we go upon him nor put upon him, except by the lawful judgement of his peers or the law of the land.

This famous declaration has been in the law books, in slightly amended form, for over 700 years. Magna Carta was confirmed by subsequent monarchs, usually at the request of Parliament, fifty-five times. It was resurrected by one of our greatest lawyers, Sir Edward Coke – 'tough old Coke, the toughest man England ever knew' – in the reign of James I and Charles I. He wrote a commentary upon it in a volume of his *Institutes* which was published by authority of Parliament in 1642, the year in which the Parliament decided to defy Charles I. The *Institutes* are the foundation of the modern law, the source to which lawyers have recourse when modern precedents are lacking or produce no clear principle. It was Coke who drafted the Petition of Right of 1628, the second of our great constitutional documents, and the arguments in Parliament on this Petition were founded on six Acts, Magna Carta itself and five Acts confirming it. The ideas of the 39th Article are implicit in the law of England as well as explicit in the books.

What is more important, though, is that the 39th Article is implicit in the behaviour of the ordinary Englishman. He is not only a free man; he is truculently free. He is, perhaps, the most law-abiding citizen in the world, particularly when the law seems to him to be sensible; but no man is more ready to take offence when the law is broken. He does not obey orders because they are given by some person in authority: he obeys orders when they are lawful orders, issued by a person who has legal authority to issue them. John Hampden, gentleman of Buckinghamshire, is one of our national heroes; and Hampden has written his name into history because he refused to pay a tax of twenty shillings, imposed upon him by the sheriff in accordance with orders from the King. He was charged before the Exchequer Chamber in the *Great Case of Shipmoney*. Seven judges found against him and five in his favour; but later Parliament reversed the verdict. The important point, though, was that Hampden refused to obey an order that he thought to be unlawful and thereby helped to establish a tradition.

Gray in his *Elegy written in a Country Churchyard* used the phrase 'village Hampden'. There are village Hampdens everywhere, and city Hampdens, too. Every man in Britain is a Hampden, for he will not be 'pushed around' by any Jack-in-office. His wife, probably, will be even more articulate, for she usually has an excellent flow of language; but it is not necessary to say very much – "'Ere, chuck it, mate', is all that is needed. In a Police State the law is regarded as an instrument of governmental control, a series of commands laid down by the governors for the governed. In England more than elsewhere the law is attuned to social convention, for it has grown with the people and therefore has both grown out of and into their customs. Hardly anybody, except the professional lawyer, pretends to know what the law is, but everybody knows what is right and wrong, and this vague conception is not very far from a popular generalization of the law itself. The police constable's standard remark. 'Hey, you can't do that there 'ere,' is expressive of one aspect of this popularized law, but so is the obvious answer, 'Ho! can't I, and 'oo says so?' There speaks the cockney Hampden. Nor is it wholly, or even usually, what the policeman says. 'I'll 'ave the law on 'ee' is another aspect of it; and off she bounces to the police station to lay a complaint before a sympathetic sergeant. If the sergeant is not sympathetic enough there is always the justice of the peace: but neither policeman nor justice can cow the defendant if she thinks she has the law on her side. '*Nullus liber homo* . . .' applies to the female of the species.

There is, of course much more in this idea than a mere assumption that one must obey lawful orders and refuse to obey unlawful orders. There is the idea of freedom itself, and this deserves a little investigation. There has been so much intermarriage in the last thirty generations that almost every man may regard himself as the descendant of serfs, for 800 years ago most of the common people were serfs. They were not slaves, liable to be bought and sold and completely under the orders of owners. A slave is, or may be, outside the law, a piece of property, a 'chattel'. A serf was tied to the soil, which was owned by the lord, and he had to perform services to the lord; but he had rights as well as duties. Those rights and duties were laid down by the law, which determined every man's status and the consequences that flowed from it. Even the King himself was bound by the law. Henry de Bratton, commonly known as Bracton, who wrote our first systematic law book about 1250, said (in Latin) that 'the King ought not to be under man, but under God and the law.' He did not mean what we mean, the law applied by the King's judges in the King's courts. He meant that there was a customary law which regulated the rights and duties of every man, be he King of England or lowly serf. What King John had done – or, at least, what he was said to have done – was to break this customary law, and so the leaders of the Church, the barons, and the representatives of the City of London forced him to approve Magna Carta, in which he promised to maintain their rights and incidentally (in the 39th Article) the rights of free men generally.

The 'free men' of Magna Carta did not include the serfs, but the principle was the same. The King had rights, the barons had rights, free men had rights, and even serfs had rights; and nobody might infringe these rights. The peculiarity of England (which it did not even share with Wales and Scotland) was that these rights came, by a process of evolution, to be enforced by the King's judges in the King's courts and to be protected by the law which those courts developed, the general or common law of England. When Coke resurrected Magna Carta all men were 'free men' in the sense of the 39th Article. There were no longer feudal lords nor serfs, but different people had different rights in land, and some had no rights in land at all. As subjects of the King, they all had rights which it was the duty of the King's courts to protect.

The fundamental question in the seventeenth century was whether this common law applied to the King himself; and this was an important question because, though by this time every man was a 'free man' and there were no slaves or serfs, he might still be 'pushed around' by the King or the King's officials. What John Hampden claimed was that Charles I had no legal right to compel him to pay twenty shillings. Though seven judges found against him, not one of them declared that the King was above the law and could do exactly as he pleased. Even Chief Justice Finch, who went as far as he dared, merely said that the King had certain rights which could not be taken away, even in Parliament.

PARLIAMENTARY SOVEREIGNTY

One cannot keep Parliament out of the story, though its function was to make law and not merely to see that it was observed. The King of England was never an absolute monarch. Not only had he to observe the feudal law, like everybody else, but also he was bound by that law to consult his great men – his barons – whenever he wanted to do something unusual, like making war or raising special subsidies. Magna Carta itself had said – though this clause was not repeated after 1215 – that the King should not levy 'scutage or aid', other than the customary aids, except by the 'common counsel of the realm'; and to take that counsel he had to summon the archbishops, bishops, abbots, earls, and greater men (barons) singly, and the rest of the King's tenants by writs addressed to the sheriffs.

This did not mean that the Great Council had a fixed membership. The King had to summon – and indeed wanted to summon – all the really great men when he had something important to discuss; but he could, either on such an important occasion, or on a minor occasion, summon anybody whom he wanted present. If there was trouble in Yorkshire, the way to deal with it was to ask the sheriff to get a few knights elected as representatives in the county court, and they came to Westminster – or wherever the King happened to be – to answer for the men of Yorkshire. If the king wanted information, advice, or financial assistance from all the counties he could ask all of them to elect knights. As early as 1213 John summoned four knights from each county 'to discuss the affairs of the kingdom'. In 1254 Henry III summoned two knights from each shire to grant an aid. In 1265 Simon de Montfort went further: in the King's name he summoned not only two knights from each county but also four to six burgesses from certain towns. His purpose was not to set a precedent but to obtain support against the barons, but he did in fact set a precedent. Edward I on several occasions followed his example and summoned the knights and burgesses to a 'parliament' at which weighty matters, like the raising of money for a war with Scotland, were discussed. To the Parliament of 1295, for instance, there were summoned, in addition to the great men, two knights from each shire and two burgesses from each borough. From then until 1832, whenever it was desired to summon such a parliament there were two representatives from each of the communitates (in Latin), or the communes (in French, which was the legal language) or the commons (in English).

The Commons did not sit with the King and his lords. When the King wanted their presence they were summoned to the Bar; and from the fourteenth century, if not before, they were told to elect a Speaker to speak for them. If they chose to have a meeting to discuss what the Speaker should say on their behalf, that was their business. Indeed, when they had to give sanction to some sort of levy to raise funds they had either to sit together or in groups – the knights in one and the burgesses in another. The significance of this arrangement was that when they had these meetings the Commons could discuss not merely what the King had put before them in what we now call the King's Speech, but any common grievances that they had; and if they wished those grievances met by action by the King they could put up a petition or, in Law Latin, a *billa* requesting the King to enact the necessary laws. From the reign of Henry V they went even further: they put their *billa* in the form in which they wished it enacted.

In the two centuries which elapsed between the accession of Edward I in 1272 and the accession of Henry VII in 1485 the old feudal nobility, the great barons who held lands of the King and provided him with the knights and men-at-arms for his armies, virtually disappeared. The Wars of the Roses, which arose out of the conflicts among the descendants of Edward III, finished off the process. Meanwhile the landowner as such was becoming important because the value of English wool was discovered. The towns, too, throve on the wool trade. The Commons of England, the 'landed interest' in the counties and the burgesses in the cities, became more and more important. The serfs became free peasants and agricultural labourers. This process developed apace when the Tudors brought internal peace and security. On the other hand, the Tudors were too able to allow this 'middle class' to come in conflict with them. The strength of Henry VIII and Elizabeth I lay in the fact that they had the middle class behind them. Elizabeth had some trouble with her parliaments, but she knew how to handle them. The conflict came when James VI of Scotland became James I of England.

The conflict was perhaps inevitable. The landed interest was becoming too powerful to play a subordinate role. It was willing to assent to the proposals of Henry VIII, and accordingly that king usually exercised his powers in Parliament. It was not willing to accept everything proposed by Mary I, and even Elizabeth I managed to get what she wanted only by the exercise of consummate judgement. James I and Charles I had not the same skill; but they required even greater skill, because under the Tudors the Commons had learned their power and men like Coke, Eliot, Pym, and Hampden were not to be browbeaten. Neither monarch was fitted by character and experience to wage a contest with the combination of county gentlemen and common lawyers which dominated the Stuart Parliaments.

The fundamental issue was the relation between King and Parliament. Elsewhere in Europe the feudal kingdoms were turning into absolute monarchies. In England the feudal restrictions on royal power were being converted, at least according to custom, into parliamentary restrictions on royal power. We are apt to think of the Civil War as a conflict over religion. Certainly there were strong theological opinions on both sides: but most of the country gentlemen were not interested in ritual, vestments, and dogma. Parliaments had acquiesced in the breach with Rome under Henry VIII, the Protestant Reformation under Edward VI, the restoration of Roman Catholicism under Mary I, and the modified Protestantism of Elizabeth I. What concerned them was not that James I had religious views of his own but that he claimed power to give effect to them without parliamentary sanction. There were other aspects of the matter: the House of Commons was anti-papal because it was nationalist; it was anti-clerical because the landowners and the merchants disliked the assumption that an ecclesiastical ceremony gave the clergy (most of whom were uneducated and of low social status) the right to pronounce on matters of personal conduct and business relationships.

Nevertheless, the real question, as the parliament men and common lawyers, who were in alliance, saw it, was whether the King could make laws outside Parliament. Historically and legally the King had quite a good case. It never had been true that legislative power was vested exclusively in Parliament. In *Bate's Case* the judges held that the King had power to levy import duties without consent of Parliament, and in *Hampden's Case* that he could levy ship-money. Against the precedents cited by Coke and Selden supporting the authority of Parliament could be marshalled a respectable collection of precedents supporting the authority of the King. The middle class came down on the side of Coke and Selden because they felt instinctively that the King's claim threatened their liberty and their property. When under the Commonwealth the control of Parliament – or what was left of it – became tyrannical the middle class welcomed the restoration of the Stuart monarchy.

The Civil War settled that the King was not above the law. He had only such powers as the law allowed him: and the common law could be amended only in Parliament. Later it was decided that James II had no power to suspend the law or to dispense with it in any individual case, though he could pardon an offender once he had been tried and convicted. The Civil War did not, however, settle the question of religious liberty. The idea of religious toleration is not easily accepted. If one's own beliefs are not mere versions of truth but Truth itself, then those who deny those beliefs are heretics, believers in and supporters of falsehoods. Moreover, it was not just a question of tolerating the heresy of one's next-door neighbour but also a question of tolerating the heresy of one's king or queen. Can one render allegiance to a heretic? This in turn made it even more difficult for monarchs to tolerate heresy in their subjects. Logically – and when Philip of Spain sent the Spanish Armada against England with the blessing of the Pope it was not mere logic – heresy and treason went together.

The notion that Roman Catholics were potential traitors died hard, for after the accession of George I in 1714 there was a Roman Catholic claimant to the throne, whom many believed (probably correctly) to be the son or the grandson of James II and therefore, under the laws of hereditary succession, better entitled than George I and George II. Bonnie Prince Charlie suffered his final defeat in 1746 and George III, who ascended the throne in 1760, had no rival: but even in 1780 there were 'No-Popery' riots in London. Not until the present century were the last relics of legal discrimination against Roman Catholics removed, and even now a Roman Catholic cannot ascend the throne, nor can a monarch become a Roman Catholic, or marry one, without forfeiting the Crown.

Nor was it easy for Protestants to tolerate each other's interpretations of Christianity. Not all those who rebelled against Charles I were Puritans or dissenters from the Church of England, and religion was not the *casus belli*, but the Puritans feared for their religion, and their religion gave strength to Cromwell's Ironsides. The Puritans nevertheless tended to be even more intolerant; and Cromwell himself, as Lord Protector, had to reprove his 'saints' for their intolerance. 'Bethink ye in the bowels of Christ,' he said, 'and think it possible that ye may be wrong.' His secretary, John Milton, wrote the finest defence of liberty in the English language, and perhaps in any language. Even so, the restoration of Charles II was acclaimed by nearly everybody, and thenceforward the Nonconformists were the friends of toleration. They had to be, in order that they might be tolerated, for they did not again obtain political power until the nineteenth century.

Meanwhile, though, the Church of England had to become tolerant in order to retain its pre-eminence. If there had been a secession every time there was a difference of opinion there would have been not one Church but a dozen. Moreover, the bishops were appointed by the king, and a bishop who was continually warring over doctrine was a political nuisance. Men of 'broad' views, who admitted a wide latitude of opinion, were favoured. Often, indeed, they had no views at all. In the eighteenth century the landed interest was in the saddle – metaphorically as well as actually. The eldest son succeeded to the family estates and became the squire. A younger son had a choice between the Army and the Church. If the Church was chosen and the squire was politically important, the parson was marked out for preferment to a deanery if not a bishopric. Bishops, too, had seats in the House of Lords, and their political support was valuable to a Prime Minister who had no disciplined party behind him but only the 'influence' of his political friends. It mattered not whether the bishop had any theology provided that his politics were sound and his friends influential.

It is easy to be cynical about the eighteenth century, for it was cynical about itself: yet it produced some remarkable people. The story of the 'yeomen of England' is in large measure a romance, and yet the British armies which fought under Marlborough at one end of the century and Wellington at the other, and the navies which fought under Nelson early in the nineteenth century were by no means inefficient, and they certainly were not drawn from the more solid sections of the population. The people who settled North America or worked and fought with the East India Company were not all drawn from the 'landed interest'. It is no longer fashionable to have empires and 'imperialist' is a term of abuse; but imperialist adventures do require courage and endurance and energy and self-sacrifice and most of the other virtues. Britain in the eighteenth century established an Empire and, in losing it, created two nations, one the United States of America and the other Canada; and forthwith it started to build another empire. That kind of thing cannot be done only by military adventurers looking for loot and merchants looking for easy money.

Even more remarkable was the quality of work done at home by the hard-drinking, hard-riding landed interest and the middle classes of the rapidly growing cities. The hard-boiled squires stayed down on the farm, developed scientific agriculture, and built houses of great architectural merit. The Church was corrupt and lackadaisical, and yet it produced the Wesleys. The universities were somnolent and yet they produced people like Sir Isaac Newton and Adam Smith. Politics were thoroughly corrupt, and yet produced Bolingbroke and Walpole, Chatham and Pitt, Burke and Fox. Britain made profits from the slave trade, but it also stopped it. Above all, the Industrial Revolution began in Britain, not merely because it had coal and iron but also because its geniuses invented machinery and new methods of transport.

The explanations of these remarkable phenomena are no doubt many and complex. It would seem, though, that one of the explanations is that the Englishman (and, as the century developed, the Scot too) was a free man, living in an age of toleration in which anybody could think what he pleased and even do what he pleased so long as he kept within a law which was rarely illiberal – except in so far as it protected property. The pattern of his ideas, if he had any, was derived from the world's greatest literature, that of Greece. Unlike the Greeks, though, the English knew how to govern. The laws were often crude and barbaric, and yet they were, on the whole, sensibly administered by the squires as justices of the peace and admirably developed by great judges like Holt and Mansfield. Not even the incursions of the Pretenders or, later on, the threats of Napoleon interfered with the development of a material prosperity in which it was still possible to maintain a high standard of civilization.

The Industrial Revolution changed the face of England and of the lowlands of Scotland. The French Revolution of 1789, coming in the midst of a great economic development, for a time caused a reaction to illiberal ideas. Property seemed to be in peril: but more than property was in peril, for the Revolution substituted the tyranny of the demagogue for the tyranny of the aristocrat. The demagogues were succeeded by Napoleon, who was even more dangerous because he threatened invasion. The result might have been a harsher oligarchy by the perturbed landed interest. Nevertheless, the liberal ideas of Chatham and the younger Pitt were kept alive by Charles James Fox and his handful of followers; and a new power developed in the land, the power of Nonconformity, enriched by the secession of the Methodists from the Church. There was an easy transition, which lasted a hundred years, from a landed oligarchy to a popular democracy. Most of the development was presided over – though she did not always approve and regarded 'democrat' as a term of abuse – by the second of England's great queens, Victoria, who ascended the throne in 1837 when the development had just begun, saw an Empire of free peoples parade before her in 1897, and died three years later as Britain and what we should now call the Commonwealth entered the twentieth century.

DEMOCRACY

After the accession of William and Mary in 1688 there was no doubt that Parliament was supreme. The monarchs still had great influence, but they depended upon Parliament for the funds which they employed and the laws which they administered. Indeed, they depended on Parliament for their thrones. William III had only a remote hereditary title, and Mary's claim was only a little better. After the death of Queen Anne, the Hanoverian line could justify itself only by the Act of Settlement. Even now, probably, one could find a more direct descendant of James I than Elizabeth II* – even forgetting the Duke of Windsor, who abdicated by Act of Parliament.

The medieval parliaments had contained the great lords

* On strict hereditary principles, the line of Charles I takes precedence over the line of James I. The line of Henrietta, Duchess of Orleans, daughter of Charles I, being Roman Catholic, was passed over in favour of the line of Elizabeth, the Electress Palatine, daughter of James I, from whom Elizabeth II traces descent.

and the representatives of the 'commons' – the knights of the shires and the burgesses of the boroughs. The great lords had been succeeded by great landowners, ennobled by successive monarchs because of their wealth and political influence. The knights of the shires had been superseded by landowners elected by freeholders. Many of the boroughs were dominated, for purposes of elections, by neighbouring landowners. The landed interest therefore dominated the eighteenth-century Parliament. Even the wealthy merchants and manufacturers of the towns were not all enfranchised, sometimes because the urban electors were self-elected 'freemen', and sometimes because the town itself, being a product of the Industrial Revolution, had no separate representation.

By 1832, though, the balance of economic power had changed. The landed interest was still important, but the manufacturers were wealthy and influential. Sir Robert Peel, who first became Prime Minister in 1834, was the son of a manufacturer. Generally, the manufacturers were Whigs and Nonconformists, and it was not until a section of moderate Tories joined the Whigs in 1830 that reform could be effected. Even then William IV had to threaten to create fifty Whig peers in order to get the Bill through the House of Lords.

The Reform Act of 1832 enfranchised the middle class of the towns and effected a balance between town and county more closely reflecting the balance of economic power. Immediately, its consequences were barely noticeable and the landed interest continued to dominate politics until the repeal of the Corn Laws in 1846 – which had helped British agriculture by keeping up the price of wheat but necessarily kept up the price of bread also, and therefore the wages paid by the manufacturers. The fusion of the Whigs and the Peelites, who had repealed the Corn Laws, led to the creation of the Liberal Party, based primarily on the manufacturing interest and 'the Nonconformist Conscience'. The rump of the Tory Party, ably led by Disraeli, was based essentially on the support of the 'country gentlemen' or landed interest: but the distinction between land and other forms of property was fast disappearing as urban rents made up for the losses caused by the repeal of the Corn Laws. Disraeli gradually weaned the Conservative Party, as it now called itself, from insistence on 'protection' for agriculture so that it could appeal to the growing volume of urban voters. In 1867 Disraeli went further by enfranchising the householders of the urban working class. Though the Liberals thought that the urban workers would vote Liberal, Disraeli thought that many of them would vote Conservative, especially if he gave them the vote. Disraeli was right, but not right enough. The Liberals were in office from 1868 to 1874 and again from 1880 to 1885. In that second period they enfranchised the householders of the counties, and so gave representation to the rural working class. This almost coincided with a split in the Liberal Party and, except for one short interval, the Conservatives were in office from 1886 to 1905. They were no longer based on the landed interest, whose influence had almost entirely disappeared. After 1885 what was called 'Society', the wealthy, educated minority, was almost solidly Conservative and the Conservative Party also had a large volume of working-class support. Meanwhile, though, the trade unions were developing, and in 1899 they (with a few Socialist groups) formed the Labour Representation Committee from which the Labour Party sprang. For the time being this Labour influence came down on the side of the Liberals and helped to give them the enormous majority of 1906.

There was no change in the franchise until 1918. By that time the Liberal Party had split, one section, led by Lloyd George, joining with the Conservatives (and with Labour support) to form the Coalition Government of 1916. The Act of 1918 based the franchise not on householding but on residence, and therefore gave the vote to all persons resident in the constituency on a fixed date, the minimum age for men being 21 and that for women (who were given the vote for the first time) being 30. In 1928 the Conservative Government reduced the age for women voters to 21, and in 1948 the Labour Government removed certain cases of double voting.

The franchise is now based on the principle of 'one person, one vote, one value'. Every person of full age, not subject to a legal disqualification, resident in a constituency for a short period, has the right to vote in that constituency, and in that constituency only. The voting is no longer done in 'communities', the counties and the boroughs, because the counties and the boroughs are divided into constituencies of approximately equal size, though in the more sparsely-populated fringes in Wales and Scotland some attention is paid to area as well as the population; also, the distribution in 1948 was not quite exact. In principle, though, a vote cast in Acton has the same weight as a vote cast in Midlothian.

It must not be thought that democracy depends only on a broad and equal franchise. It depends also on the efficiency of the machinery of government in reflecting public opinion as shown by the ballot box. Even Queen Victoria, at the beginning of her reign, thought that the stability of a Government depended on her support. After she married the Prince Consort in 1840 she began to realize that the nature of the Government depended not on her but solely on the majority in the House of Commons. This did not stop her from using her influence for the Conservatives late in her reign, but even when she disliked and distrusted Gladstone she had to take him as Prime Minister, because he led the Liberals and the Liberals had a majority. It must be remembered, too, that the House of Lords was and still is part of Parliament. Early in Queen Victoria's reign it lost the power to change the Government, and now it cannot even obstruct legislation for more than one year. The result is that when a Government loses its majority in the House of Commons it goes out of office forthwith, as Mr Attlee's did in 1951 and Sir Alec Hume's in 1964.

Even these characteristics do not, by themselves, make Britain a true democracy. What does make it so is more easily sensed than explained, but clearly it is bound up with the idea of liberty. There are certain obvious characteristics. The whole procedure is honest. A person who is entitled to be a voter will find his name on the register; or, if it has been

accidentally omitted, he can have it put on. If his name is
on the register he will be able to cast his vote in complete
secrecy, so that no one will ever know – except possibly a
High Court judge in a formal legal proceeding – how he
voted. He can be sure that his vote will be counted, and on
the side on which he cast it. He can be sure, too, that only
genuine votes will be counted. These things cannot be said
of all countries.

The elector also has a choice. In practice it is a choice
between two lines of policy, the one Labour, the other
Conservative. Sometimes there are other choices, Liberal
or Communist or Scottish Nationalist or Independent.
Anybody can start a party and anybody can get nominated
as an independent. In practice, though, electors prefer to
vote for a party which has a reasonable chance of forming
a Government, and so the smaller parties and the indepen-
dents tend to get pushed out. Also, there are constituencies
which are persistently Conservative or persistently Labour –
the 'safe seats' – so that an elector in the minority seems
always to be beating his head against a blank wall: his only
consolation is that in other constituencies his political
friends will be in a majority. With all these qualifications,
however, there is a free choice. He can vote for the Government or against the Government, without fear that he will
be prejudiced or victimized. Britain can go communist or
fascist if it wishes to do so; communist or fascist countries
cannot go democratic – in our sense of the term – because a
liberal democrat cannot become a candidate, nor could
anybody vote for him if a candidate dared to deny the
orthodox doctrine.

Nor is this all. The mere fact of having a choice is useless
unless it is possible to learn what the choice is. In Britain a
person can listen to and talk about any ideas he pleases; he
can read a book or write a book about them; he can publish
or subscribe to a newspaper or a periodical dealing with
them; he can issue posters containing slogans about them
or he can put such posters in his windows; he can organize
or attend public meetings at which such ideas are expounded;
he can even ask for and obtain police protection to prevent

disturbance; he can go to meetings at which different ideas are expressed and heckle the speakers; he can argue in the pub or the club, the bus or the tram, the train or the café, the street or the park. He is, in short, a free man, entitled not only to the personal liberty which has been read into Magna Carta but also to political liberty. There are, or may be, communist newspapers and fascist newspapers, communist books and fascist books, communist meetings and fascist meetings, communist organizations and fascist organizations, communist processions and fascist processions: but in communist and fascist countries there are no newspapers, books, meetings, organizations, or processions supporting liberal democracy.

Even this does not tell the whole story. It has been said that the Englishman is not only free but truculently free. That is true in politics also, and there freedom goes much deeper, for it creates a tradition of free enquiry which enables ideas to develop and expand. Few of us are very original in our thoughts. We are educated to a set of conventional ideas. We tend to speak the same language, practise the same religion, wear similar clothes, follow the same social conventions, read the same newspapers and books, and generally follow the same paths as our neighbours. Indeed, we inherit a social tradition from our ancestors which we hand on to our children, without much change or development. It is even true that there are class ideas which we derive from our economic status. If we own property we assume as a matter of course that the protection of property is a fundamental political need; if we produce goods for export we are convinced of the advantages of free trade; if we produce for the home market we are likely to favour 'protection' for home industries; if we are university lecturers or school teachers we realize the importance of education; if we are skilled workers we are strongly in favour of full employment and perhaps also of nationalized industries; if we are poorly-paid unskilled or semi-skilled workers we not only support the skilled workers but also consider that the State must provide social security. On the other hand, it is wrong to consider these economic interests only, for it is not true that the British worker or even the British employer thinks purely in economic terms. The reader knows that his religion, the ideas that he inherited from his parents, the ideas that he discusses with his friends, the ideas that he obtains from his reading, and even the ideas which he works out for himself, are frequently against his economic interest. Those who agitated against and finally abolished the Slave Trade – to take one example – gained nothing from the process except the sense of satisfaction which comes from the performance of a social duty. To suggest that Christian marriage is the product of economic self-interest is nonsense. Even the communists exhibit the falseness of the doctrine, for most of them belong to the middle class which would have to be 'liquidated' when communism arrived.

There are, however, other factors. Where the standard of living is exceedingly low and education is obtainable only by the wealthy, the most important liberty of all, freedom of thought, is of little value because there is little material on which thought can build. The common people of Britain were in that position a hundred years ago, and that same position is still to be found in many parts of the world. Even now the education which we give to the mass of our citizens is so inferior that they cannot make adequate use of the knowledge open to them. Their level of intelligence is represented by the crime column, the women's page, the novelette, the football pool, and the Hollywood film. Freedom of thought is therefore not a particularly valuable principle to them, for they have not learned to think.

With all these qualifications, the freedom of thought which is implicit in our tradition is fundamentally important. Most of us most of the time accept conventional ideas, but we can break away at any moment, and a minority does. Where there is a set of ideas which have to be accepted, which are taught in all the schools, and which can never be denied, there can be no progress, because all ideas have to circulate within an iron framework. The glory that was Greece was due to the fact that the Greeks were a free people; the revival of learning in the Middle Ages was due to the impact of Greek ideas on a small educated public which had begun to think for itself; the great Elizabethan age was due to the creation of a small middle class which had learned to think; England in the eighteenth century produced remarkable men and women because it was a free country. Nor has any British subject any cause to be dispirited in the difficult conditions of today. Those of us who are overseas see these things more clearly than those who stay at home. English is only one of the languages of the world, and yet most of the new ideas come to us in English. The people of Britain are only one section of the English-speaking peoples, and yet most of the ideas expressed in English come to us from Britain. The rest of the free world does indeed contribute; but the label 'Made in Britain' is a guarantee of quality deriving from a long tradition of freedom.

What democracy has done in Britain is to increase its potential. We have still to make full use of freedom of thought, because many of us – including the author – are still in the third or fourth generation of literacy. Nor must it be considered that this freedom affects only those problems which come into political controversy. Poetry and prose, literature, art and architecture, music and the drama, are the more important products of freedom of thought.

THE TYRANNY OF THE MAJORITY

It was inevitable and, in the ideas of most, desirable, that the extension of the franchise should lead to a greater measure of social and economic equality. The new electors, like the old, had a social status to defend – it was never true that the common people 'had nothing to lose but their chains' – but they had more to gain than to lose. The Liberal Party at first and the Labour Party during the present century led the demand for radical reforms; but in order to win votes the Conservative Party had to follow suit, and indeed it is evidence of Disraeli's political acumen that he saw the need more clearly than Gladstone.

It is relevant, too, that social and economic change has

been very rapid in the past two centuries, chiefly because of the exploitation of deposits of coal and oil through the invention of the steam engine and the internal combustion engine. Change may be even more rapid in the future if the scientists learn to control atomic energy and the peoples of the world learn to control themselves and their politicians. The changes which have already taken place have altered the face of Britain. The population has multiplied and has collected into large towns where life has to be regulated much more closely than in the country, where services like transport, gas, water, electricity, and drainage have had to be provided on a large scale.

The task of adapting the laws and the system of government to meet the demands of electors and the changes brought about by economic development has fallen to Parliament. The volume of legislation passed in a single session is now far greater than the volume of legislation passed in a whole Parliament in the eighteenth century. To the older Ministries have been added Ministries for Health, Local Government, Air, Agriculture, Education, Labour, Food, Supply, etc.

This extension of the ambit of the law has raised in a new form the problem of the relation between law and liberty. It has always been true that there could be no liberty without law; for if everybody is free to do as he pleases there is no liberty for anybody to do as he pleases. John Smith is free to walk down the High Street to the Arctic Café to buy an ice-cream soda because the law forbids the obstruction of the highway and assault and battery, provides a medium of exchange, regulates sales, and does its best to guarantee the purity of ice-cream. The liberties necessary for the working of democracy, the right to vote, the right to organize, the right of free speech, the right of assembly, and so on, are all products of the law. On the other hand every law is a restriction of liberty. Hence a balance has to be struck between law and liberty. Much of the modern law is designed not to impose restrictions but to provide services through State action. Incidentally, though, restrictions on liberty have to be imposed. The problem has been to find

out where the law should end and liberty begin.

The law of education may be taken as an example. Its primary purpose is to make education available to every child. When the urban working-class was enfranchised in 1867 Robert Lowe, a leading Liberal politician, said that 'we must educate our masters'. Democracy implies an educated electorate. For the ordinary elector, however, the real purpose of the law of education is not to teach him how to vote but to enable his sons and daughters to obtain suitable jobs. Perhaps, indeed, he may go further and agree that the real purpose is to enable his sons and daughters to acquire the satisfying emotions that come from knowledge and understanding.

When the State provides education, though, must it force every child to attend school? If so, for how long? Moreover, must the child attend a State school or may he attend a school chosen by the parent because of its religious teaching, its academic standard, its games facilities, or its snobbish appeal? Should the child of rich parents have better education than the child of poor parents because the rich parents can afford to pay for it?

These are not easy questions to answer, and different people supply different answers. In almost all fields of legislation there are similar problems. Nor are they always the subject of party conflict. Ought broadcasting and television to be controlled by a monopoly, or should everybody be allowed to butt in? Liberty in this field, it will be noticed, means liberty to those who have large funds and those who have large funds are those who have something to sell at a profit. Our liberty, therefore, may have to be an advertiser's liberty.

CHAPTER 2 : *The Queen*

THE QUEEN

GOVERNMENT is not purely a matter of logic. Few of us are such stern realists that we cannot be affected by emotion. When we are asked to cast a vote we do not send for the *Statistical Abstract of the United Kingdom* and start drawing graphs. It matters not a jot that Shakespeare was an Englishman and not a Czech or a Pole, but we are pleased that he was born in the very English town of Stratford-on-Avon. Everybody loves a Queen, particularly if she appears to be charming. Even her name, Elizabeth, sets up a chain of emotions, for we have learned to revere 'Good Queen Bess'. Those of us who have even the scantiest recollections of history think of Shakespeare, and Sir Francis Drake, and the defeat of the Spanish Armada.

Even the constitutional lawyer cannot ignore these emotions. Analysed coldly, however, the functions of the monarchy may be said to be four. First, appearing in an impersonal fashion as 'the Crown', the Queen's name is the cement that binds the Constitution. Secondly, the Queen's name similarly binds the units of the Commonwealth. Thirdly, there are political functions of the highest importance which the Queen performs personally. Fourthly, the Queen is a social figure exercising important functions outside the political sphere.

THE CROWN

When

> Paddy wrote a letter to his Irish Molly O!
> Saying 'If you don't receive it write and let me know'

what exactly did he do? Those were the good old days, before anybody had heard about 'inflationary spirals', and so he bought a penny stamp, stuck it on the envelope, and dropped the envelope into a pillar box. Let us analyse the process.

Paddy went into a post office provided by the Crown, and controlled – remotely – by the King's Postmaster-General. He took from his pocket a copper coin issued by the Royal Mint and bearing the King's head. It was, by order of the King in Council, a token of value. Twelve copper pennies were worth one King's shilling, and twenty shillings were worth, significantly enough, one golden 'sovereign'. Paddy handed the penny to a supercilious young lady – who was rather conscious of the fact that she was a servant of the King – and asked for a penny stamp. He received in exchange a piece of adhesive paper with the King's head on it. Having stuck the stamp on the envelope, he dropped the envelope into a pillar box marked 'G.R.' for 'Georgius Rex' and thereupon, though Paddy did not know it, his letter became the King's property. It was collected from the box by a servant of the King called a postman, and was handed over from one servant of the King to another until at last it reached the hands of a postman in Tipperary – and in those days he was a servant of the King, not of the Republic of Ireland – who dropped it into Molly's letter-box. The King had delivered Paddy's letter, it had ceased to be the King's property, and it had become Molly's property, though in accordance with laws made by the King in Parliament the contents were Paddy's copyright.

King George V knew nothing whatever about Paddy's letter, and yet the whole transaction was carried out in his name. England used to be a feudal lordship owned, in the peculiar feudal sense, by William the Conqueror. The Norman kings and their successors extended their control over the country and gradually the feudal law and local customs were superseded by the King's law. The laws were made by the King with the assent of Parliament, and they were enforced in the King's courts. The King levied taxes through his royal officers, with the consent of Parliament, and purchased property. The King's justices saw to the maintenance of the King's highways, along which ran the stage-coaches proudly bearing the legend 'Royal Mail'. The number of the King's servants increased rapidly, and today many of them must feel very remote from the Queen because they are appointed by royal officers, who are appointed by royal officers, and so through a long chain of command to the Postmaster-General, who really was appointed by the Queen or her predecessor.

This is one example of many. What in other countries is regarded as the property of the State is in England the Queen's property, the property of the Crown. The public service is the Queen's service, the service of the Crown: even income-tax demands are sent to us 'On Her Majesty's Service'. Contracts made with Government departments are contracts with the Crown. The Queen, not the State, prosecutes criminals, and the cases are called as 'The Queen against John Doe'. In itself, all this is of no great importance. It is lawyer's shorthand. 'The Queen' or 'the Crown' could quite easily be replaced by 'the State'. Yet this personification of the State has some psychological effects, because it is not always easy to distinguish the personality and the institution. At the highest level of administration the Queen herself is involved. When the Metropolitan Police was under severe criticism for inefficiency and corruption, a retired officer was asked to become Commissioner of the Police for the Metropolis. He did not want the post because he had just accepted a remunerative appointment. He was told that the King wished it, and he then accepted, because his conception of duty did not allow him to refuse to obey 'the King's Command'.

Not many believe that their work for the public service is known to the Queen; and yet there is something more personal in serving the Queen than in serving the State. The older generation will remember the recruiting poster of the first World War: 'Your King and Country need you'. The State is amorphous: the Queen is real. When we toast 'The Queen' we do not try to distinguish the person and the institution. We can actually see the Queen if we feel so disposed. She drives down to Parliament in a State coach; she actually reads 'the Queen's Speech', though we know she did not write it. It is a little easier to put aside our private interests in order to serve the Queen than it is to put them aside in order to serve the State.

What is more, it is not easy to distinguish between the State and the Government. So great is the difficulty that in some countries it is treason to oppose the Government. In a democracy we may, and often do, criticize and even oppose the Government, though from the best patriotic motives and for the best of all reasons, that we believe the Government to be wrong. There are times when the politician has to speak for the nation, but usually he speaks for his Government and his party. Even the President of the United States is a partisan, a Democrat or a Republican, and nobody ever forgets that 'Mr President' is L. B. Johnson. In Britain we have no difficulty in distinguishing between patriotism and party loyalty; the one is towards the Queen, the other towards the party. We can 'serve the Queen and damn the Government'.

Still that is not all. The United Kingdom is a union of three kingdoms, England (and Wales), Scotland, and Northern Ireland. It is more accurate in fact, though less accurate in law, to describe it as a union of four countries, England, Wales, Scotland, and Ulster. The people of the United Kingdom have discovered that it is not wise to ignore local loyalties. Long ago Edward I sought to appease the patriotism of the Welsh by making his infant son their Prince. After Bonnie Prince Charlie and his Highland supporters were defeated at Culloden in 1746 the Scots were sullen and resentful: the Earl of Chatham found the real solution: he formed the Highland regiments of the British, Army and sent the clans to fight for George III. The Welsh have retained their language and the Scots their law. The United Kingdom is, indeed, a remarkable kingdom. It has no national language, because nobody is required to speak English. It has no national flag; for though the union flag was formed by the juxtaposition of the crosses of St George (for England), St Andrew (for Scotland), and St Patrick (for Ireland), nobody is compelled to fly it except Her Majesty's ships, which fly it at the jack (whence, 'Union Jack') and also quarter it in the white ensign (i.e. the English flag) at the stern. Whenever the Queen is present the royal standard, which quarters the arms of England, Scotland, and Ireland, is flown: but when the Queen is not in residence the Cross of St George is flown at Windsor Castle, the Cross of St Andrew at Holyrood Palace, and the Dragon of Wales at Carnarvon Castle.

The people of the United Kingdom, too, have no common name. They are Englishmen, Scots, Welsh, and Ulstermen, and most of them are never quite sure which they are because there has been so much intermarriage. They are all British subjects, but so are Canadians, Australians, New Zealanders, South Africans, Indians, Pakistanis, Ceylonese, Chinese from Hong Kong and Singapore, Fijians, and a great many Africans from the back of beyond. Then they have no national anthem. True, they think they have, but 'God Save the Queen' is a royal hymn which does not mention the United Kingdom at all and is sung wherever men serve in the Queen's name. To hear a national anthem an Englishman has to go to Twickenham or Wembley and listen to the Welsh football crowd sing (most tunefully) 'Land of our Fathers'. The English, of course, join in, though they are really more at home with that treasonable song 'Will you no' come back again', by which the Scots plead with Bonnie Prince Charlie to come back and turn the descendant of George II off her throne.

The people of the United Kingdom made one big mistake; they did not manage to persuade the Southern Irish to keep both their loyalty to Ireland and their loyalty to the successors of George III. There were perhaps faults on both sides, but the essential fault was a defect in the system of toleration as it applied in the eighteenth century. That century was tolerant of everybody except Roman Catholics, and the Southern Irish were Roman Catholics. William Pitt was great enough to realize that things must be different in Ireland, but George III was not. Then the Irish Parliament was suppressed by as blatant a piece of corruption as even the corrupt eighteenth century could show. That grievance was made worse by the great potato famine of the hungry forties, and most of the Irish left to become policemen and politicians in the United States of America. Perhaps Gladstone's Home Rule would have solved the problem, but he lost his majority in 1886 and the 'Unionists' were not willing to concede it until 1921, when it was too late. By that time the Irish had learned to serve Ireland and not the King, so that eventually, in 1949, Ireland became a republic – less Ulster, which remains loyal – even aggressively loyal – to the Queen.

That bad mistake apart, the peoples of the United Kingdom have performed a remarkable feat. They have maintained unity in diversity. As we discovered in 1940, we can trust our own people; and yet they are not our own people; they are Englishmen and Welshmen, Scots, and Ulstermen. Indeed, we must not forget that some of them are not of the United Kingdom at all. There are Manxmen and Jerseymen, men of Guernsey and men of Sark. Most of us speak English, but some prefer Gaelic or Welsh or Norman-French. Now all this can be done in a republic, if need be. The constitutional lawyer can, by appropriate drafting, solve any constitutional problem if people are willing to accept a solution. If they are in conflict over 'ideologies' there is no solution. The characteristic of British constitutional development has been its tendency to let fundamental issues work themselves out. The existence of the monarchy has enabled this to be done. The person who thinks primarily in terms of the United Kingdom can serve the Queen because she is Queen of the United Kingdom. The Scottish nationalist who thinks primarily in terms of Scotland can serve the Queen because she is Queen of Scotland. He can wave the Cross of St Andrew because the Queen herself does so, and nobody asks him to wave the Union flag; he can talk Gaelic to anybody who is prepared to listen, because 'the Queen's English' is not forced on anybody and Gaelic is as much a 'national language' as English; he can sing 'God Save the Queen' with fervour because she is Queen of Scotland. What is more, the Englishman will go along with him on St Andrew's night, toast both the Queen and the 'land o' cakes' in the dew of the mountains, dance a reel or two, and wind up the evening with 'Auld Lang Syne'. The monarchy is a useful instrument because it is personal and flexible, real and tangible.

THE QUEEN AND THE COMMONWEALTH

'The Crown' has performed the even more remarkable feat of converting an Empire into a Commonwealth of independent nations. Incidentally we have mentioned above the Isle of Man and the Channel Islands. They have remained under the Crown and yet retained their own legislatures. When Englishmen (and Scots) made the perilous voyage across the Atlantic they, too, established, and were authorized to establish, their own legislatures, but they remained subjects of the King. Unfortunately that obstinate monarch George III got into controversy with his American subjects over the right of the Parliament of Great Britain to tax them. History now tells us that, to use the popular phrase, it was 'six of one and half-a-dozen of the other'. The result in any case was the tendentious, inaccurate, but extremely well-written piece of propaganda called 'the Declaration of Independence'. Thirteen of the American colonies became the United States of America with a republican Constitution: but there were other colonies in what we now call Canada and the West Indies. To them were added colonies in Australia, New Zealand, South Africa, Ceylon, East and West Africa, Malaya, and the Pacific Islands. India was never a colony, and on the whole it was treated with rather less imagination than the colonies – or perhaps with too much imagination and too little realism. The mistake of George III was, however, never repeated. When Lord Durham was sent in 1839 to report on the constitutional problems of Canada, he said, in effect, that if a colony had its own legislature, it had to be allowed to govern itself except in matters of imperial concern. There were people in Britain who did not see how this could work, but it was really simple enough. The Queen could appoint Ministers for the United Kingdom, but she could also appoint Ministers for Canada. The Queen's Ministers in the United Kingdom could accept responsibility for matters of imperial concern and the Queen's Ministers in Canada could accept responsibility for matters of Canadian concern. In due

course the matters of imperial concern diminished to
nothing. The King's Ministers for the United Kingdom were
responsible for the policy of the United Kingdom and the
King's Ministers for Canada – which now stretched from
sea to sea – were responsible for the policy of the Dominion
of Canada.

The essential link was, until recently, the monarchy. To
say that the Queen is Queen of Canada is not quite correct.
She is Queen of all the territories that admit allegiance to
her; she is one Queen and not a score of queens. This may
read like metaphysics, but in fact metaphysics has been
avoided. The Queen is a person and not an institution, and
so she is one Queen. She has a score or more of governments,
governing in her name. Of these nine are independent of
each other – the United Kingdom, Canada, Australia,
New Zealand, Ceylon, Sierra Leone, Gambia, Jamaica,
Trinidad, and Malta. The rest are controlled, in greater or
less measure, by her Government in the United Kingdom.

The common relationship to the Queen is called 'allegiance', but what it means in practice is not very easy to
explain, for it differs in different parts of the Commonwealth. Generally speaking it means that a citizen of a
Commonwealth country is a 'British subject' or a 'Commonwealth citizen' – the terms are interchangeable – but what
that means depends on the local laws. In Britain a 'citizen
of the United Kingdom and Colonies' has no greater rights
than any other British subject: in other Commonwealth
countries he may be virtually an alien.

Until 1949 it was relationship to the Queen which determined membership of the Commonwealth. The idea of
'the Crown' had proved to be as flexible outside the United
Kingdom as it had been inside: and this is still so where the
Queen is part of the Constitution of a Commonwealth
member. Normally she acts, outside the United Kingdom,
through a Governor-General, appointed by her on the
nomination of the Government concerned. Usually he is a
prominent local citizen – a Canadian in Canada, a Ceylonese in Ceylon – who acts as a constitutional monarch
for a period of five years or more. Though he acts without

consulting the Queen, he sends regular letters to her. She thus becomes familiar with the prominent personalities and the political problems of the country concerned and can talk intelligently about them when visitors call at Buckingham Palace or she visits the country. When she does the latter, the Governor-General is temporarily super-seded, for the Queen is as much at home in Ottawa or Colombo as she is in London or Edinburgh. In most other respects, too, the formalities are observed. 'God save the Queen' is not a national anthem but a royal hymn, and can be sung wherever her writ runs. There is a Royal Canadian Navy, a Royal Australian Air Force, and so on. In some of the countries the mails are royal mails and the roads are the Queen's highways, while official letters are sent 'On Her Majesty's Service'. Ministers and civil servants are servants of the Crown. Writs are served in the Queen's name, the Queen prosecutes criminals, witnesses can give Queen's evidence, and judges give judgement in her name.

One disadvantage of this form of Commonwealth is that every one of its units must be a monarchy. Before Britain proved that a monarchy could also be a democracy – a proof supported by Belgium, the Netherlands, Denmark, Norway, and Sweden – it was thought that a monarchy was undemocratic. Even Joseph Chamberlain, before he became a Unionist, was a republican. It happens that the leaders of the Indian National Congress were brought up on Victorian political ideas, and so the Indian Constituent Assembly established a republican Constitution. It is not a very con-vincing document, for it is of a monarchical type. Instead of having a Governor-General appointed by the Queen on the recommendation of the Prime Minister of India, there is a President elected by an electoral college. From the point of view of machinery the result is exactly the same. Dr Rajendra Prasad would have been Governor-General for five years; he was actually President for five years. The real difference is in the intangibles. India uses the word 'Union' or 'State' wherever another Commonwealth country would use 'Queen' or 'Crown'. Possibly that is an advantage, for the idea of 'India', except as a geographical expression, is a

very recent development in the long history of Asia.
Perhaps the idea of union should be emphasized in order to
offset disintegrating tendencies in a population so vast and
so diverse. On the other hand the idea of monarchy is
essentially Indian – in the neighbouring island of Ceylon,
which shares the later part of the same history, the Queen
is the latest of a line of monarchs which started a thousand
years before there was an England – and it is a much simpler
idea than that of an amorphous, elusive, and intangible
India. The Queen can have her picture in the papers;
nobody has ever seen, or ever will see, the Union of India.

The issue was decided, as most political issues are, not by
logic and experience but by emotion. Queen Victoria had
proclaimed herself, with Disraeli's approval but against his
better judgement, as Queen-Empress of India. Unfortunately it proved to be as bad a name as that given to the
proverbial dog. In Asia if a person was objectionable, he
was described not as a fool, a knave, or a cad but as an
'imperialist'. What is more the Congress politicians who
fought for the freedom of their country, and now rule India,
were necessarily opponents of the King-Emperor. British
rule was the King-Emperor's rule: and so not only had the
Emperor to go but the King too. On the other hand the
Congress politicians were sensible people, realists like most
Indians: they saw some advantages in being in the Commonwealth and not many disadvantages. Hence the Pro-
visional Government of India informed the Government of
the United Kingdom that India proposed to become a
republic but wished to remain in the Commonwealth. This
upset the pundits, who had been saying flatly that the
Crown was the link that kept the Commonwealth together.
The Prime Ministers of the Commonwealth, including
India, were invited to Whitehall, and they brought their
pundits with them. The Prime Ministers agreed forthwith
that India might break the link but maintain the connexion, and the pundits were told to put that into a formula.
Actually the Government of India, no doubt in consultation
with the Government of the United Kingdom, had already
supplied the essential phrase. In relation to India the King

was to become 'Head of the Commonwealth'. With that phrase all His Majesty's Governments could agree. The difficulty was that they wanted the Head of the Commonwealth to be King also in relation to them. The problem was, therefore, so to draft the formula that those who preferred 'the King' to 'the Head of the Commonwealth' should be as satisfied as those who preferred 'the Head of the Commonwealth' to 'the King'. A great many pundits' heads were scratched for the next thirty-six hours, but they came together eventually and produced an agreed formula.

One must not exaggerate. The links which bound the members of the Commonwealth were far more substantial than the rather hypothetical link of the Crown. India proved it by wanting to stay: but the story shows how important is that extraordinary flexible implement which the politicians and constitutional lawyers of England – for once it is England and not the United Kingdom – have devised. India's example has been followed by Pakistan and by several countries in Africa.

THE QUEEN IN PERSON

If the Queen knew about everything that went on in her name she would be almost omniscient. Every day hundreds of thousands of people are acting in her name and millions are having dealings with her representatives. The Queen personally is not aware of it, but on the very morning on which this was written she received several letters from the Vice-Chancellor of the University of Ceylon. He was, for instance, very anxious to know whether the electric current which she had promised to supply by July would be enough; he also asked when he might expect a reply to a letter asking about the installation of telephones; he would be grateful if she would move certain furniture and clean the floors before he ordered university furniture to be put in; and so on. That kind of thing is constantly going on from Limehouse to Wagga Wagga.

Generally the Queen is 'the Crown', the legal abstraction. If one starts exploring the stream of political action, however, there is always the possibility that one will come upon the Queen in person, real flesh and blood. Amid the millions of pieces of paper circulating 'On Her Majesty's Service', one will be found signed with the Queen's own hand - the 'sign manual', Elizabeth R. Even that may be a fiction, for it may be a mere facsimile, printed under legal authority to save her time and energy. Nor is it always easy to say when the Queen in person will be involved, for it depends primarily upon her energy and range of interests.

One thing clearly she must do. She must make certain that she has a Government in the United Kingdom. Incidentally she has to make certain that she has nine or more other Governments in the Commonwealth, but this she does by deputy; and, besides, we must not confuse the story, like Charles Dickens, by trying to tell ten stories at once. We are so accustomed to the idea that the day Sir Alec moves out of 10 Downing Street, Whitehall, S.W.1, Mr Wilson moves in, that we forget how this remarkable coincidence occurs. 'The King's Service', said the Duke of Wellington in 1834, 'must be carried on'; and so he took the reins of government while Sir Robert Peel was posting home from Rome in what the newspapers would now call the 'record time' of nine days. In relation to this particular function the Queen in person must see that the Queen's Service is carried on.

This is usually an easy task. When in 1964 we heard the last (or almost the last) of the election results come over the wireless, we all knew the necessary consequence. Sir Alec would go to Buckingham Palace and tender his resignation; the Queen would thank him for his services and ask him to remain in office while she, the Queen, made other arrangements; the Queen would then send for Mr Wilson and ask him to form a Government; Mr Wilson would not be surprised by the request, but for the sake of the record he might go away to consult his friends; and back he would go to accept office. The task was simple because the Constitution had supplied the answer. The Conservative Party had lost its majority in Parliament and no longer had either right or power to govern; the Labour Party had gained a majority in Parliament, and its leaders had both the right and the duty to form a Government. The fact that the task is usually easy, though, must not cause us to forget that somebody has to do it. Suppose a defeated Prime Minister did not resign? The answer is, no doubt, that the House of Commons would at the first opportunity pass a vote of no confidence. In fact, until 1868 that was the normal procedure. Suppose the Prime Minister still did not resign? The case has never happened because our political leaders always obey the rules; but if it did happen there could be no doubt about the Queen's duty: she would send a polite note of dismissal and commission the leader of the successful Opposition to form a new Government.

Even when everybody is anxious to obey the rules the task is not always easy. Though the British elector prefers the two-party system, the Ins and the Outs, there are periods of transition, like that from 1918 to 1935, when three parties are operating. If there were three parties of equal size, it is possible to have one of three types of minority government or one of three types of coalition. Nor does it follow that one of the three leaders would of necessity be Prime Minister. The Prime Minister of a coalition might well be a moderate man acceptable to both parties, rather like the Lord Aberdeen whose coalition took Britain into the Crimean War in a fit of absent-mindedness.

Again, the office of Prime Minister may suddenly fall vacant through his death or resignation, leaving the party in power without a recognized leader. The Queen then has the task not only of choosing a Prime Minister, but also, in effect, of choosing a party leader. It may not be an easy task. Politicians like actresses prefer to have their names at the top of the bill and, again like actresses, they can be very temperamental. There may also be constitutional issues involved. On the resignation of Bonar Law in 1923, George V had to find a Conservative Prime Minister. Several of the Conservative leaders were in Opposition, for they had supported Lloyd George at the break-up of his coalition. The choice lay between Baldwin, who had had only a very short Cabinet experience, and Lord Curzon, a peer, not as popular as he was able, and the victim of an undergraduate rhyme which made him 'a very superior person'. The King decided, after consulting several elder statesmen, that, with the Labour Party as the main Opposition, it was desirable that the Prime Minister should be in the House of Commons. This excluded Lord Curzon, who was by no means pleased with the decision.

A problem which arose in South Africa in 1939 might easily arise in Britain. The Prime Minister disagreed with his colleagues in the Cabinet over an issue of great importance – the declaration of war. Instead of resigning he advised the Governor-General to dissolve Parliament, evidently expecting that, after the election, he could reconstruct his Government more to his way of thinking. The Governor-General thought this an abuse of the King's prerogative of dissolution, and refused to accept the advice. Thereupon the Prime Minister resigned, leaving to the Governor-General the task of finding a new Prime Minister, a task which in this instance proved to be easy.

These examples show that the Queen is no mere figurehead. She does not steer the ship, but she has to make certain that there is a man at the wheel. Nor is it always easy to know when the problem will arise. Neville Chamberlain in 1937 had a large majority, but by 1940 George VI was looking for a Conservative Prime Minister who could secure Labour as well as Conservative support – and found him in Mr Churchill.

It is however true that the cases are exceptional. Normally the machine runs efficiently because the Government has a majority and, if it loses it at an election, a Government will be formed by the Opposition. If the Queen chooses to let the machine run she can do so. Except in Army matters Edward VII was not very interested in the problems of government, and so his Prime Ministers – Balfour, Campbell-Bannerman, and Asquith – tended to forget him. If, on the other hand, the Queen is as conscientious as her father or Queen Victoria she can exercise considerable influence.

In the long run, of course, the policy of the country must be determined by the party in power, but it is far from being

the case that the party policy determines the line of action
without discussion or debate. It is not a question of turning
on one of two taps, marked respectively 'Conservative' and
'Labour'. The process is much more like that in a chemist's
shop, where almost any concoction can be made, whether to
kill or to cure. What is more, the Cabinet has to write the
prescription. The problem of government, it has been said,
is the problem of choosing the better of bad alternatives.
The Cabinet's choice is not necessarily the best, even when
it has had the assistance of the civil service and the writers
of leading articles. If the Queen chooses to read the documents and keep herself informed in other ways, her advice
may well be worth listening to. For most politicians the end
of the road, at least for the present, is the next general election: the Queen can afford to look beyond and to point out
that a solution which seems the best in the short run may
be the worst in the long run.

Capacity to advise depends primarily on an odd quality
called 'judgement'. It is not often associated with academic
brilliance or political popularity. It is indeed often the
product of a rather slow-moving mind. The man who jumps
to inspired conclusions often forgets one-half of the problem.
The popular orator has often finished his speech before he
has thought out what he ought to say. The good solid citizen
who has assimilated a long experience and conscientiously
studied every question as it arises is more likely to be right
than the virtuoso. What is usually wanted is sound common
sense, and in politics that is rarer than its name would
suggest.

To say that Queen Victoria possessed this sort of judgement would be an exaggeration. She was quite often swayed
by her emotions, as Disraeli knew when he played upon
them. On the other hand, she lived a truly Victorian life of
virtuous toil. Towards the end of her long reign she had
been longer 'in politics' even than that sprightly and (as
some thought) incorrigible old man William Ewart Gladstone. What is more , while Gladstone had sometimes been
'in' and sometimes 'out', she had been 'in' since the age of
eighteen; and she had a remarkable memory. Of her

successors George V and especially George VI had something of the same capacity for hard work and a capacity for judgement above the average. To have such a person at the centre of affairs, cool, calm, and judicious, is a great advantage, especially with a brilliant but wayward Prime Minister.

It must be remembered that the Queen has on her table nearly all the documents that go to the Prime Minister. A person who has the responsibility for decision is apt to read them more carefully than one who has not; but every administrator knows the tendency to think out the consequences and reach a conclusion even when somebody else has the responsibility. If the reader has been a careful student of daily newspapers and weekly reviews for twenty years his mind will have moved away from the slogans which all parties use and which induce him to lay down the law in the home or the pub or the club. The Queen has not one newspaper a day but dozens of them, carefully marked by her staff so that her attention may be drawn to the more significant items. She also has more weeklies and monthlies than a public library. To all that must be added every confidential document that goes to the Cabinet and some that do not, every blue book and white paper, the letters from ambassadors and Governors-General, the talks with distinguished men and women who are invited to dine and sleep, and so on.

If only a fraction of this material be digested, the Queen can make herself one of the most learned people in her Commonwealth. What is wanted, though, is not so much learning as a capacity to understand the nature of a problem. The real difficulty of government is to take a decision which may have profoundly important consequences. Its elements mill round in one's head until they begin to sort themselves into a pattern. If while this process is going on one can 'think aloud' in the presence of one who has the same problem in his head the process of sorting out becomes much easier. To sleep on a problem is always helpful, because the refrain which seems to dominate the orchestra to-day may have diminished in volume tomorrow; but the same result can be achieved today by talking to a person who hears a different refrain. Last time we had a Queen, Walter Bagehot said that the monarch had the right to be consulted, the right to encourage, and the right to warn. That is not quite what happened under George VI, and it probably is not happening under Elizabeth II. To express a doubt is often more helpful than to formulate a criticism; to throw in a casual remark is often more helpful than to write a memorandum. The easy personal relationship that George VI maintained with his Ministers probably had more influence than the letters which Queen Victoria wrote in such profusion.

THE QUEEN AND THE COMMON MAN

Our newspapers are full of politics for several reasons. One is that politics affect millions of people, another that politicians like their names in the papers and so provide plenty of 'news', and a third is that it is easier to report a dull speech in Parliament than a witty speech in the 'Rose and Crown'. The most popular newspapers, though, feature the 'human interest' and believe in the newspaperman's story that 'the way to kill a paper is to put politics into it'.

This general attitude to politics is really very sensible. One of the great advantages of a free country is that one can think about politics – if at all – only in odd moments. One can glance at the front page and say 'what a rotten Government this is' (no matter which Government) and turn to the more interesting items on the sports page. It would be different if a chance remark might bring the Gestapo or the Ogpu to the front door. Then one would have to be like the wise old bird:

> There was an old owl who lived in an oak
> The more he heard the less he spoke;
> The less he spoke the more he heard;
> Now wasn't he a wise old bird?

The notion that the Russians spent their lives in thanking God (or Beelzebub) for Stalin is probably a piece of propa-

ganda. Doubtless they spent most of their time, like other
people, in trying to forget about politics.

The truth is that the better the world is governed the less
we think about politics. The best things in the world are
rarely done by politicians. There is little merit in making a
speech, unless it is a very good one; there is greater merit in
writing a book, painting a picture, reading a poem, singing
a song, kicking a goal, scoring a try, hitting a century, or
doing anything else really well. The ordinary sensible fellow
would rather have a meal, go to bed, see a film, or fill up a
football pool, than listen to a speech. This is said to be the
age of the Common Man; but the common man does not
like capital letters and what he really wants is to be left
alone. He gets hot and bothered about politics when something goes wrong. He is, however, very willing to do his duty
once every four or five years, and turn out to vote, and once
or twice a day he casts his eyes over 'what them politicians
is a doing of'.

In short, the citizen is citizen for an hour or so a day. The
rest of the time he is an employee, the father of a family, a
follower of the Arsenal, a churchgoer, and a student of
racing form. The man next door, though, may be a scientist,
a poet, a philosopher, or even an author. If the fellow down
the street will insist on talking politics he is a bore to be
avoided. If he happens to be a Marxist he will be not only
a bore but a fool, for he will think that football pools have
been organized by the capitalists to draw attention away
from the need for bloody revolution. To him the Spurs and
the Arsenal – as their names show – are instruments of
American imperialism.

Now the Queen comes into this, for she spends a great
deal of time on ceremonies which have nothing to do with
politics or are only remotely connected with them. Possibly
the inspections of units of the Royal Navy, the Army, and
the Royal Air Force may be said to have something to do
with politics, though when Christopher Robin went down
with Alice to see the Guard at Buckingham Palace, Alice
really was not trying to indoctrinate him with imperialist
ideas. (On the contrary, 'A soldier's life is terrible hard',

said Alice.) It can hardly be said, though, that a visit to a coal mine or a university, a speech to the British Association for the Advancement of Science, the drive up the course at Royal Ascot, a front seat at a 'command performance' or a cup final, a charity ball or a subscription dinner for Distressed Gentlewomen, are acts of high political significance.

What in fact the Royal Family tries to do is to take an active part in and give encouragement to those efforts of ordinary people which achieve merit. It is concerned as much with religion, art and literature, learning and sport, commerce and industry, as with politics. Naturally the Queen cannot shake hands with fifty million people, but in the course of her reign she will be seen by millions and speak to thousands, and most of the thousands will have done something worth while.

In this context 'honours' must be mentioned. Old-fashioned republicans dislike titles, or at least some titles. Apparently they are considered to create class distinctions. In fact, though, the distinctions exist already. When a philosopher, a poet, a musician, a cricketer, or a trade union leader is given a knighthood or an O.B.E., the explanation is that those who advise the Queen consider that he has acquired merit in his particular sphere of action. The title itself gives no claim to distinction; what matters is the reason for the title. The United States at one extreme and the Soviet Union at the other issue medals and awards. There is no harm in them; indeed, like prizes at school, they encourage people to do good work. Certainly they are less objectionable than the large and gaudy cars by which so many try to demonstrate their superiority. The advantage of the British system is that the Queen is associated with the award, so that the person who receives an O.B.E. is shown to the world to be a person who has been thanked by his Queen for his services to the community. If the standard of award is maintained, the more O.B.Es. there are the better the community is served. What is more, we need this kind of service. The passenger, the sort of person who is content to rub along, is no doubt a very estimable person, but we do need our Shakespeares and our Sullivans, our Bacons and our Byrons, our Newtons and our Nelsons, our Turners and our Tennysons, our Wellingtons and our Wordsworths.

In spite of all the recent difficulties, the standard of attainment in Britain is high. There are great poets, philosophers, scientists, artists, architects, scholars, social workers, novelists, dramatists, and so on, in other countries. Certainly Britain has no monopoly: it is doubtful, though, whether any country can show so high a level of attainment in so many different fields. These things matter more than material resources or power. One Shakespeare is worth a thousand atomic bombs – though, significantly enough, there would have been no atomic bomb but for British scholarship. One of the Queen's most important functions is to help to maintain this high level of attainment among the peoples of the United Kingdom.

CHAPTER 3 : *Politics*

*

THE IMPORTANCE OF POLITICS

To give a just appreciation of the part which politics plays in the life of the community is not easy. The politician always exaggerates it because it increases his importance. On the other hand those who think in terms of culture and scholarship tend to minimize it because, in the long view, the politician is merely playing with symbols. His influence on the course of events, though profound in the short term, is shallow in the long term. Already people have almost forgotten that there was a Hitler. In the first World War there was a famous recruiting poster in which the postwar child was made to ask: 'What did *you* do in the Great War, Daddy?' We now know what question the postwar generation did ask: 'What Great War was that, Pop?' In a few years time, Smith Minor will be telling us how Kaiser Hitler I tore up the scrap of paper and hurled his tanks at the contemptible little army. It is true that Smith Minor's view of history ought not to be taken very seriously, but by 2050 we shall know whether Hitler or, say, T. S. Eliot had the greater influence. Possibly the history books will record that the greatest event of the second World War was the discovery of D.D.T.

That kind of remark helps to give us perspective, but those of us who can look back forty or fifty years do realize how much our lives have been affected by politics. This is mainly because of the upheavals of two wars. If we consider our daily life in peacetime we shall be inclined to the view that politics is not very important, and that the less there is of it the better. That attitude, too, is dangerous. In some environments it leaves politics to crooks and gangsters, in others to megalomaniacs like Hitler, and in yet others to paranoics like the average communist. We cannot justly complain of the little wisdom with which the world is governed if we neglect to apply wisdom to government.

On the whole the compromise which Britain has adopted

is a sensible one. Politics in the main is the concern of people who 'like that sort of thing'. In every generation a few persons of ability take to politics, while the level of intelligence and experience among Members of Parliament, though not high, is above the average for the country. A Cabinet does not contain as able a group as, say, the Senate of a University, but it has a broader experience. In the civil service, too, it has advice from professional administrators of skill and experience and some of the best of the technical experts. Though it would be impossible to say that any Government was adequate to its task, it is not easy to say how a better could be devised; and it is certainly better than those produced in most other countries.

POLITICS AND THE SOCIAL CLASSES

One feature of importance is the remarkable homogeneity of the peoples of the United Kingdom. This may seem strange in a kingdom which is not one country but four, where three languages are spoken, where there are three different systems of law, and in which religious differences are quite substantial. It is nevertheless true. The United Kingdom is a densely populated country with an integrated economy and an excellent system of communications. Any slight economic change, such as a fall in textile prices or under-production of coal, is immediately felt everywhere else. Its dense population and good communications, combined with complete adult literacy and a fairly high standard of living, enable its popular newspapers to secure the largest circulations in the world. Probably half the population watches television news. All this does not mean that there are no differences of opinion, but it does mean that such differences have to occur within a common framework of knowledge and experience. The technique of lying and distortion, which is used by politicians everywhere, and especially by those who accept the principle that the ends justify the means, has to be used with discretion in Britain, because so many of the matters that arouse political controversy are based upon factors of which the elector has personal experience. It is possible to tell the elector that the Soviet Union is a paradise or a slave State, for he has never been there; it is futile to tell him that he has nothing to lose but his chains, because he knows that he has a houseful of furniture and that the house itself will be his property when he has finished his payments to the building society. In fact, the whole argument for the class war falls on stony ground because it does not accord with the ordinary voter's experience. It may have been possible to divide the people of Britain a century ago into the 'bosses' and 'the people'. It may still be possible to do so in some parts of the world. It is not possible in Britain because there is a gradation of classes from the comparatively poor (who would be described as 'middle class' in Asia) to the comparatively rich (who would not be regarded as rich in the United States). The range of net income is wider than in countries like Denmark but narrower than in countries like the United States and the Soviet Union. The ordinary voter does not know this, but he does know that from the unskilled labourer to the managing director there is a gradual rise in incomes, and there is no point at which a line can be drawn between the capitalist and the proletariat. The unskilled worker is a bit of a capitalist and the managing director is a wage-slave.

Another important feature of the British class system is the large proportion of people who are neither among the comparatively poor nor among the comparatively rich. They are sometimes spoken of as 'the middle class', but that is a confusing term because it tends to be associated with social behaviour rather than with income. A skilled worker, for instance, tends to think of himself as 'working class' while a clerk or a teacher or an insurance agent tends to think of himself as 'middle class'. Economically, however, these groups overlap. The best-paid skilled workers earn much more than the worst-paid clerks and teachers. What is more, the skilled carpenter or bricklayer or mason may find it easier than the clerk to become a 'boss'. He may set himself up as a master carpenter, say, and take small contracts. If he does well he may find himself employing other carpenters and even plumbers, bricklayers, and masons. In short the carpenter becomes a 'building contractor'. It is not very easy to decide at what point he ceases to be one of the 'workers of the world' and becomes a 'b—capitalist'. The clerk with the secondary-school education, on the other hand, remains an employee; he may ultimately become a manager or a director, but he is always dependent upon his salary.

The effect of industrialization and mass-production has been to create huge commercial and industrial units employing large numbers of salaried employees. How it has come about can be seen very easily by watching the conversion of the master carpenter into the building contractor. The master carpenter does everything himself with the assistance of his 'mates'. He makes the contract with the contractor; he orders the materials; he pays the wages; he buys the tools; and he takes off his coat and collar and does the job. As his business expands he has to set up an office and employ clerks and assistants; he opens a workshop and employs a staff; his specifications are drawn up by a technical staff; he employs quantity surveyors to determine what materials are needed; his solicitors draw up the contracts; and so on. In due course he converts his 'firm' into a private company and, if it still prospers, into a public company. The Morris bicycle-shop in Oxford became eventually the Nuffield Group. This has been a general tendency for a century and more. The master craftsmen have been superseded by limited companies employing not only unskilled and skilled workers but also clerks, assistants, quantity surveyors, engineers, mechanics, lawyers, shop managers, and so on. There has been the same tendency on the commercial side. The little shop has tended to be superseded by the chain store employing large office staffs, shop assistants, shop walkers, maintenance staff, and so on. One aspect of this development is very obvious. There is a large demand for young men and women educated in the secondary schools, the great majority of which did not exist in 1900.

There is no doubt that a person's economic interests

influence his political views. The unskilled worker tends to favour expanded social services, minimum wages and limited hours of work, food subsidies, and other devices for keeping down the prices of essential commodities, rent restriction, cheap housing, etc. Nor does it matter to him that these policies require heavy taxation, for he considers that such taxation should fall on the wealthy. The wealthier citizen wants almost exactly the reverse. His primary concern is to keep down taxation, and therefore he desires 'economy' in the public services. If he owns shares in companies – and as incomes rise the value of the shares held rises more or less proportionately – he will also be interested in profits and will tend to object to measures which limit them.

It may be noted that the fiercest controversies of politics do not come into this contrast at all. Home Rule for Ireland had no economic motivation in Britain. In the early years of the movement the Irish Home Rulers were usually tenants, while the Unionists (outside Ulster) were usually landlords. Gladstone at first interpreted the problem as one of land reform; but he proved to be wrong. Not only economic interests but also emotions (strengthened by religious differences) were involved.

Again, the great debate between free trade and protection was not due entirely to a direct economic motivation. It was due in part to a difference of opinion over the effects of tariffs. It was alleged by some that tariffs increased the cost of living, and by others that they increased wages. The Liberals emphasized 'cheap bread', while the Conservatives emphasized 'more employment' and 'higher wages'. Both, it may be noted, were appealing to the manual workers and lower-paid 'white-collar workers'. There was, however, also a difference of opinion among manufacturers and the commercial interest. Those whose profits depended mainly on the home market were anxious for protection to 'keep out the foreigner', while those whose profits depended mainly on the export trade thought that protection would increase the cost of production because the prices of raw materials (e.g. cotton and wool) would rise, or because the cost of machinery and other home-produced articles would rise, or because wages would rise to meet the higher cost of living. Thus, the controversy between protection and free trade was in reality a controversy between two comparatively wealthy groups, each of which produced arguments to persuade the ordinary voter.

Further, socialism is not necessarily a matter of controversy between the richer and the poorer. 'The nationalization of the means of production, distribution and exchange' does not necessarily make the poor richer. In itself it does no more than convert the employees of limited companies into civil servants. The shareholders receive Government stock instead of industrial or commercial shares, and if the compensation is adequate they receive the same average incomes. The community is richer only if the nationalized monopoly is a more efficient producer or distributor than limited companies in competition with each other. On this basis the controversy is limited to the theme of the respective efficiency of nationalized monopolies and free competition. There are, of course, other factors. Some believe that the shareholders should receive lower incomes or no incomes at all even if, to take the case which is put by those who defend free competition, they happen to be widows or aged persons whose savings have been invested in shares. Others point out that the industry (e.g. the transport industry) can be organized for service instead of for profit. Yet others stress the immorality of what they call 'the profit motive'. In any case the controversy is not over socialism, as such, but over the consequences of socialism. What happened in fact was that the trade unions were persuaded by the Fabians that socialism would benefit the industrial workers, while the Conservatives have sought to persuade them that free enterprise would benefit them more.

The way in which these controversies developed showed the importance of the economic motive. Conservatives, Liberals, and Labour politicians were agreed that what we now call the Welfare State was demanded. The parties vied with each other to produce more and better social services. They disagreed over free trade, but both sides appealed to the manual workers on the assumption that they were interested mainly in the standard of living. They have also disagreed over socialism and have appealed to the manual workers on the same assumption. In the last fifty years, however, and especially in the last thirty years, there has been a new factor, already mentioned, the growing strength of the so-called middle class, the clerks, mechanics, shop assistants, insurance agents, and white-collar workers generally. So numerous and influential has this class become that it has held the balance of power.

If the reader lives in a large town he can work this out for himself. Because the prevailing wind comes from the south-west, the residential quarter, where the bigger houses tend to concentrate, is at the west end. It is almost always a safe Conservative seat. The centre of the city and the areas to the east of it are those in which the poorer workers live, usually in terraced houses or newer municipal housing estates; they are almost always safe Labour seats. The doubtful areas, which are apt to change their allegiance, are those in which the small three-bedroomed, semi-detached houses tend to congregate – the clerks, mechanics, shop assistants, etc. In 1931 these 'marginal' constituencies went Conservative (or 'National'). In 1935 they were still Conservative, though the majorities were lower. In 1945 they went Labour. After 1951 they were generally Conservative, but in 1964 they tended to swing to Labour.

Let us be plain what we mean. It is not suggested that a manual worker always votes Labour, that a salaried manager always votes Conservative, while a clerk or a shop assistant belongs to the 'floating vote'. It is the constituency, not the individual voter, which is Conservative, Labour or marginal: but this characteristic of the constituency depends upon the assumed economic interest of the class that is dominant in the constituency. Though many manual workers vote Conservative, a manual workers' constituency is generally Labour: clerks and shop assistants are no more fickle than other people, but they are more equally divided politically, and so a swing of opinion swings the constituency.

There are, too, other factors. By implication we have

already modified the purely 'class' interest. Economically the skilled worker and the clerk belong to the same group. Emotionally they tend to belong to different groups. After some hestitation the 'craft unions' of the skilled workers allowed themselves to be absorbed into the 'trade unions' dominated by the unskilled workers. In the nineteenth century their common opponents were the 'bosses'. With the growth of huge corporations, including those controlling nationalized industries, 'the boss' as such tended to disappear. Even so, the tradition remains. The skilled and unskilled workers support the union, which supports the Labour Party. There are, however, variations. The miners, the railwaymen, and the iron and steel workers have been more 'unionist' than the textile workers and the agricultural workers, who work in smaller units. South Wales, Durham, and South Yorkshire are solid for Labour, but Lancashire and the rest of Yorkshire tend to 'swing'.

Though the clerks and the teachers are on the same economic level as the skilled workers, they usually (excluding, for instance, the railway clerks) regard themselves as salaried employees belonging to the middle class. Bodies like the National Union of Teachers and the National and Local Government Officers Association regard themselves as non-political, and their members are politically divided. The idea of social status is not another aspect of economic status; it is a separate idea.

Another emotional factor is introduced by religion. As a rough generalization one may say that the Church of England is upper middle class, the Nonconformist churches are lower middle class, and the Roman Catholic Church is working class. This excludes the great mass of the working class, who may be described as 'Cowper-Temple Christians'. The phrase is used because the agreed syllabus of religious teaching in the public elementary schools was negotiated between Lord Cowper on behalf of the Nonconformists and Archbishop Temple on behalf of the Anglicans. The great mass of the people are vaguely Christian, and religion does not affect their voting. The Church of England and the Church of Rome are conservative organizations – the small

'c' will be noted – but the Church of Rome (in Britain) is
dominated by the Irish, who have a radical tradition, and
so the areas where the Roman Church is strong (e.g. in
Liverpool and Glasgow) tend to be Labour seats. The nonconformist Churches have a long radical tradition which
made 'the Nonconformist Conscience' the backbone (if the
mixture of metaphors be permitted) of the Liberal Party.
Even to-day the 'Celtic fringe' in which Nonconformity is
strong – Cornwall, North Wales, and the North-West of
Scotland – provide most of the Liberal votes. Generally
speaking, though, Nonconformity has gone Labour, which
often seems to be more radical than socialist in consequence.

All this seems to suggest that the result of an election is
pre-ordained, and that candidates and party leaders and all
the ballyhoo have no effect. In large measure that is true.
Some seats are always Labour, some are always Conservative, while the marginal seats are fickle. They were Conservative in 1931, Labour in 1945 and (more doubtfully)
in 1964, but Conservative in 1959. Obviously we have to
study the marginal seats.

It has already been suggested that most of these seats are
dominated by the lower-paid groups of the middle class.
Economically they are on the same level as the skilled
workers, socially they are associated with the salaried
employees. Hence they are divided: but why do they swing?
We must note first that at every election a new batch of
voters, young men and women, come on the registers.
Sometimes they follow the family politics. More often,
though, they react against it. In the period after 1931, youth
was swinging to the left; after 1945 it was swinging to the
right. Secondly, we must notice that important political
group, the non-voters. They vary, over the whole country,
between 15 per cent and 20 per cent of all the electors.
Some are ill; some away from home; some 'don't 'old with
politics'; some think that politics is a dirty game; some
cannot conscientiously support either party; some just cannot be bothered. The size of this non-voters' party depends
in large measure on the success of electioneering. If it were
not for the ballyhoo it would be much larger. The posters,

the meetings, the television talks, and the leading articles create an interest. It becomes a sporting contest, surpassed only by the Derby, the Cup Final, a Test Match, and the Boat Race. The voters who are brought out in this way are obviously not very strong partisans. Some students of political form place nearly all of them among the 'floating vote' discussed below. This does not seem to be correct, however. When 'the missus' is persuaded to go to the trouble of making herself respectable and going round to the poling station, she generally votes the same way as her husband, i.e. (in this instance) Labour. If the very respectable landlady is persuaded that her savings are in danger she votes Conservative. In fact, there is some evidence that a high poll favours the Conservative Party. The potential non-voter becomes a voter because he wants to put a stop to the 'nonsense' propagated by the more radical party.

Finally, there is the 'floating vote'. 'Swinging vote' would be a better term, because it designates those who vote one way at one election and swing to the other side at the next. Its size is a matter of controversy. Some say it is as large as 10,000,000 who count 20,000,000 when they swing, because if a Conservative candidate has a majority of 4,000, and 1,000 votes are transferred to Labour, the Conservative majority is reduced to 2,000. Others say that the floating vote is only about 1,500,000, which count as 3,000,000. The difference between these two estimates may be partly one of definition. Those who give the larger estimate are thinking primarily of voters who have no consistent political philosophy, and who may be affected by the atmosphere of the moment – the relief from slaughter in 1918, the depression and its consequences in 1931, the reaction against austerity in 1945. The lower estimate is given by those who are interested not so much in why a man votes as in how he votes: if it seems to him to be the sensible thing to vote Conservative, though he cannot say why, he is not a floating voter but a safe voter.

It would seem that the lower estimate is more correct. Certainly there are millions of voters who could not give a coherent explanation of their political views. They are

Conservative or Labour at the general election just as they
are Oxford or Cambridge in the Boat Race. People make up
their minds as young men and women. They may change
sides later on, but very few can be said to 'float', in the sense
that in one election they vote one way, swing to the other
side next time, and then swing back at the third election.
Very often, in fact, the swing is rather slow; there is an
interval when the elector deliberately refrains from voting
because he cannot conscientiously vote either way.

So far we have said nothing about the candidates, and the
reason is that they do not matter much. The truth of this
observation could be judged from the two-member constituencies between the Wars. Each elector could cast one vote
for each of two candidates, and so each party put up two
candidates. There was never any great difference between
the two Conservatives, or the two Liberals, or the two
Labour candidates. Obviously one of the two must have
been a better candidate than the other, a candidate with
greater ability, or a more affable candidate, or a better
speaker, or somebody with a great many personal friends
locally. Where there was a difference it was never very
great, but it was due to local influence. The elector said in
effect: 'I usually vote Labour, but X is a local man and I
know he's a good man, so I will give him one of my votes'.
Not once were these votes numerous enough to affect the
result. If the swing was to the right, two Conservatives were
elected; if it was to the left, two Labour candidates were
elected. If this was so in the two-member constituencies, it
must have been so in all constituencies. People voted not for
the candidate but for the party.

The emphasis on the marginal constituency produces
another important feature. To win an election a party has
to win enough of those marginal constituencies. Each of the
parties has its solid backing of safe seats. It cannot lose them,
nor can it win the safe seats on the other side. Naturally it
must not lose the support of its solid supporters. If the
Labour Party annoys the miners the Communist Party will
step in; if the Conservative Party annoys the residential
suburbs a new party might be formed on the extreme right –

though that is less likely. If the miners want to influence policy, though, the Labour Party must win a majority, and that means that it must win many of the marginal constituencies. If the people of the residential suburbs are to influence policy, the Conservative Party must win many of the marginal constituencies. Hence both parties are appealing to the marginal constituencies and, in those constituencies, to the voters that can be captured.

If the election returns be analysed, it will be found that the number of votes to be captured is small. Except where the swing is considerable, as in 1931 and 1945, a difference of one million votes, spread throughout the country, would change the Government. This applies not only to 1952 or 1950 but even to 1935. In fact in 1935 the figure was 750,000. The marginal constituencies in which the swing matters are, as we have seen, the lower middle-class constituencies. Both parties want those lower middle-class votes, and so both parties seek to draw up a programme to attract them and to pitch their propaganda at a suitable level. The residential suburbs probably do not think much of the National Health Service or of an expensive system of public education, nor indeed of the Welfare State in general; but they have to put up with these things because otherwise the Labour Party will get in. The theorists of the Labour Party may want to nationalize a great many more industries than they have already nationalized, but they must not carry their theories so far as to frighten the owner-occupiers of the less pretentious residential suburbs. The person who matters, to put it in London terms, is not the citizen of Limehouse or Chelsea but the citizen of Hammersmith or Wood Green. Party policies must be studied not in the books of the theorists, but in the official documents issued from Conservative Headquarters and Transport House. It will be found that, though they differ in emphasis, the difference is really not very great. The theory that socialism makes all the difference is quite incorrect, for the official socialism of the Labour Party is a very cautious nationalization of a few important industries. The Conservatives, on the other hand, do not extol the glories of free competition. When the Labour Party wanted to nationalize the mines the Conservative Party wanted to reorganize the mining industry with a view to greater efficiency.

THE TWO-PARTY SYSTEM

It is odd, though, that there should be only two parties. There is, it is true, still a Liberal Party, but it has difficulty in re-establishing itself. From time to time new parties are started, but they are sickly plants, and they soon die.

The fact that the reader has this book in his hand is probably an indication that he has rather more than the normal interest in politics. If he asks himself whether he has ever completely agreed with the policy of any party, he will probably give himself a negative answer. Most people, probably, do not read party policies. They have vague ideas, expressed in slogans, which tell them which way to vote. They are 'for' Home or Wilson for much the same reason that they are 'for' Tottenham Hotspur or 'Middlesex'. Nevertheless, there are people with ideas, and almost invariably those ideas do not accord with the policy of any party. These are active people, too, quite capable of starting parties of their own. Yet, as soon as Parliament is dissolved, they send their names into party headquarters and offer their services as speakers. For the next few weeks they will spend immense efforts on behalf of the party and if the party gets a majority their joy will be a pleasure to see – though they disagree with a large part of that party's policy.

The principal explanation is that one can get nothing done except through one of the parties. To get anything done – unless it be something non-political like the reform of the divorce laws or the protection of performing elephants – requires the support of the Government, and the Government must have a majority in Parliament. To secure a majority in Parliament the party must be large. It must be able to fight in at least half the constituencies and preferably in something like four-fifths of them. The principal explanation for the existence of the two-party system is, therefore, that we have a two-party system. The elector does not vote for a candidate or even for a party, but for a Government. He wants Sir Alec Douglas-Home or Harold Wilson to be Prime Minister. To vote for anybody who is not either Conservative or Labour is a waste of time and energy. There are of course exceptions. One may desire to have a little group of Liberals, or Communists, or Scottish Nationalists, or Prohibitionists, or Anti-Gamblers in the House, but that is not the attitude of the ordinary voter. He has to choose between Conservative and Labour. If he has an equal dislike of both he does not vote.

It may be urged that parties do split and that the old division between Conservative and Liberal has now become a division between Conservative and Labour. That is true, and it is worth while to take some examples. In 1846 the Conservative Government led by Sir Robert Peel decided to repeal the Corn Laws. We now know that Sir Robert Peel had been convinced for some time that the protection of the wheat-producing industry was undesirable. The wheat-producers, the 'country gentlemen' who formed the main body of the Conservative Party, had not been convinced either by Adam Smith or by Cobden and Bright, and so Peel's Government kept the Corn Laws in operation. Famine in Ireland caused them to change their minds. The result was a split in the Conservative Party which kept it out of power until 1874. The Peelites were at first distinct, but they were gradually absorbed in the Liberal Party and Peel's principal lieutenant and successor, Gladstone, became the great Liberal Prime Minister.

In 1885 the Liberals split over Home Rule. It is easy to understand why the right wing, led by the eighth Duke of Devonshire, went 'unionist'. In economic and social policy this right wing had become as conservative as the Conservatives. The defection of the left wing under Chamberlain is less easily understood. Chamberlain had his own scheme of devolution in Ireland, but the differences were not great enough to justify support of a Conservative Opposition which completely disagreed with his social policy. The explanation seems to be that Chamberlain was an ambitious man of strong personality. He wanted Gladstone's Government to follow Chamberlain's policy. Home Rule was the last of a series of policies accepted by the Liberals on Gladstone's advice and against Chamberlain's advice, and so he resigned. To keep his influence, though, Chamberlain had to become not merely a 'unionist' but a good 'unionist'. He therefore became the apostle of protection and imperialism. The Liberal Unionists maintained a separate organization but had electoral arrangements with the Conservatives. The result was that the Conservatives and Unionists were in office from 1886 to 1905, except for the period from 1892 to 1895 when the Liberals, in uneasy alliance with the Irish, spent two futile years. Eventually the Liberal Unionists were absorbed in the Conservative Party and one of them, Neville Chamberlain, became a Conservative Prime Minister.

The Labour Party grew up on the left wing of the Liberal Party. It was essentially a trade union party until 1918, and it had what a new party usually lacks, an organization in depth through the trade union system. Even so it would probably have remained a small minority party but for the split in the Liberal Party caused by the formation of Lloyd George's Coalition Government in 1916. This was, in the main, a personal conflict in which Liberals took sides, and (in spite of several attempts made after the Conservatives turned out Lloyd George in 1922) it was never resolved. Some of the Liberals, like Churchill and Lord Simon, found their way sooner or later into the Conservative Party. Others like Lord Haldane, Lord Addison, and Lees-Smith joined the Labour Party. The main body remained distinct, thinking that they could stage a Liberal revival. They made a great effort, and spent much money, in 1929, but they failed and gradually they have been pushed out. For all practical purposes the two-party system was restored when the 'National' Government was formed in 1931. Incidentally it may be noted that the split in the Labour Party in 1931 was one of the causes which postponed until 1945 the formation of a Labour Government with a majority. That party kept its organization in being and left the Churchill Government as a coherent and highly organized body.

Lessons can be drawn from this history. If a party splits it may be out of office for twenty years. Disraeli's principal criticism of Peel was not that he had repealed the Corn Laws but that he had split his party. Joseph Chamberlain and the Liberal Unionists split the Liberal Party in 1886, but the Chamberlains secured office by becoming good Conservatives. Lloyd George split the Liberal Party in 1916 and enjoyed six years of power but never obtained office after 1922. MacDonald split the Labour Party in 1931 and became 'the prisoner of the Tories' for so long as they were prepared to use his name in order to maintain the fiction of a 'National Government'.

If this analysis seems to lay too much emphasis upon the ambitions of politicians, the excuse must be that politicians are ambitious. Politics is one of the sweated industries demanding, not exactly blood, tears, and sweat, but hard and unremitting toil. The remuneration, considering the expense, is poor. It can be justified only in terms of prestige and power. If politicians were not ambitious there would be no politicians.

The elector is not ambitious, but he knows he is electing a Government. The Peelites were returned because they supported a Liberal Government and the Liberal Unionists because they supported a Conservative Government. The Asquith and Lloyd George Liberals remained in the wilderness, and were gradually eliminated, because they supported neither the Conservatives nor the Labour Party. The National Liberals knew on which side their bread was buttered.

If, therefore, the reader wants to form a party to forward the policy of which he approves, he knows what to do. He must form an organization in each of 600 constituencies. He must establish a headquarters in London and issue posters, pamphlets, notes for speakers, and other forms of propaganda. He must secure the support of at least one of the national newspapers. At the next election he must put up 600 candidates and persuade the electors that 350 of them are likely to be elected. Frankly, it is easier and cheaper to join the Conservative or the Labour Party.

THE QUEEN

WHEN the ordinary person speaks of 'Parliament' he means the House of Commons. A parliamentary election is an election of members to that House. A Member of Parliament is a member of that House. This usage bears witness to the predominant importance of the House of Commons, but there is also a House of Lords whose members are 'Lords of Parliament'. For the constitutional lawyer, though, Parliament is neither House nor even both of them, but the Queen in Parliament. This is purely a formal body consisting of the Queen sitting on her Throne with the Lords of Parliament sitting before her and the Commons standing at the Bar. A little history will explain how this came about.

The King of England was bound by custom to consult his great lords on matters of great importance, and so he summoned them to a 'parliament'. John, Henry III, Simon de Montfort, and Edward I, as we have seen, began the practice of summoning representatives of the 'commons' to the more important of these 'parliaments'. It soon became the practice for the 'lords' to discuss their answers to the King in one private assembly and the 'commons' to discuss their answers in another. These answers were given to the King in 'parliament', and so the formal decision was taken by the King in Parliament. The real discussions took place, however, in the private meetings of the 'lords' and the 'commons'. This was particularly true when the 'commons' developed the practice of submitting petitions or 'bills' asking for a change of the law. The Bill was in the form that the Commons desired to be enacted. It was sent to the Lords to secure their concurrence. When it had been approved by both 'Houses' it was brought before the King in Parliament. If the King approved the Clerk of Parliament said that 'Le Roy le veult' – the King desires it. If the King was uncertain – and even if he intended to refuse but thought it unwise to say so – the Clerk of Parliament said 'Le Roy s'avisera' – the King will consider the matter. As the monarchs became less and less influential, these meetings of the King in Parliament became more and more formal, while the real work of Parliament was done in the two Houses sitting separately.

Nowadays the Queen sits in Parliament only once a year, though on other occasions she is represented by Lords Commissioners. It is a very formal occasion. She drives to Westminster in a State Coach with an escort of Household Cavalry. The peers attend in their robes, and the peeresses in the gallery wear their tiaras. The Queen robes in the Robing Room and wears the Crown. She sits on the Throne and summons the Commons, who attend at the Bar headed by Mr Speaker with the mace. She reads the Queen's Speech announcing the intentions of the Government during the session. The whole thing is a 'circus' though, like most British ceremonies, it has a purpose. It draws attention to the importance of Parliament in the national life. In theory, though, the Queen lays before Parliament the matters which she wishes to see discussed. There is a similar meeting of the Queen in Parliament at the end of each session, though usually the Queen is represented by Lords Commissioners.

The only other meetings of 'the Queen in Parliament' – except the first meeting in each Parliament in which she directs, through her Commissioners, that the Commons choose a Speaker and the subsequent meeting at which the Commissioners approve the choice on her behalf – are those at which 'Acts' have to be done. The 'Bill' discussed by the Commons and the Lords is technically a petition to the Queen. It takes legal effect as an Act because it is approved by the Queen in Parliament. She therefore appoints Lords Commissioners who sit in Parliament, request the attendance of the Commons, and then declare that 'La Reine le veult'. Effect is thus given to the theory of the Constitution. Laws are made not by the House of Commons and the House of Lords, but by the Queen in Parliament.

Nevertheless, the House of Commons and the House of Lords have ceased to be merely private meetings and have become major constitutional instruments. Though formally and legally the Queen in Parliament takes the decisions, in pith and susbstance they are taken in the Houses of Parliament. When we drive past the Palace of Westminster on the top of a bus and notice the Union Jack or the light we say that 'Parliament' is sitting. Legally we are wrong, because when the Queen is sitting in Parliament the royal standard is flown. In truth and substance, though, we are right, for the House of Commons is the major part of the Parliament and, for all practical purposes, when the House is sitting, Parliament is sitting.

Nevertheless, we must not forget our history, for history has consequences. The Queen and her predecessors have sat in Parliament for seven hundred years. For all we know the Queen and her successors will go on sitting in Parliament for seven thousand years. The British Constitution – we used to call it the English Constitution – adapts itself to new conditions in every generation but its history has been continuous. At the centre of its structure has been Parliament, a different Parliament from generation to generation and yet the same Parliament, It was not Parliament that passed Magna Carta in 1215, but it was ratified in Parliament many times. Parliament has survived the Hundred Years War and the Wars of the Roses, the Spanish Armada, the Civil War, the French Revolution and Napoleon, Karl Marx and the Russian Revolution, Hitler and the anti-intellectual counter-revolution. What more it will have to survive we do not know, but part of the strength of Parliament lies in the belief, which we hardly bother to express, that Big Ben and his successors – for Parliament will survive even Big Ben – will go on tolling the hours until the end of time.

The predominance of the House of Commons is a recent development though, like every development in Britain, it has its roots in history. The Lords completed their destruction in the Wars of the Roses and, though a new nobility developed under the Tudors, it was the House of Commons that fought Charles I. The Tudor reigns covered a period of great economic development which gave power to the landowner and the merchant. The rebellious Puritans of the

Stuart reigns were members of this new middle class, the Pyms, the Hampdens, and Cromwells. It was they who put the House of Commons in the forefront of Parliament. In the eighteenth century, it is true, the power of the Lords rose again. The great landowners were also great lords, and their influence spread even into the House of Commons. In the main, though, they left the task of governing to their henchmen, and this was particularly true at the end of the century, when Pitt and Fox went to what we should now call the top of the bill. Even at this stage, though, the House of Commons was still thought of as a private assembly. It was unlawful to publish its proceedings. Dr Johnson who made the Members speak rich Johnsonian language, reported – if that is the correct word when he was not present – the proceedings of the House of Commons as the proceedings of the Senate of Lilliput.

After the Reform Act of 1832 the authority of the House of Commons rapidly increased, for the Government depended not on the support of a few great lords but on that of a rapidly expanding middle-class electorate. Sir Robert Peel gave an indication of the change when, in his famous Tamworth Manifesto of 1834, he told his constituents, and through them the people of the country, what the policy of his party would be if it obtained a majority. Nor was there any difficulty about publishing the proceedings of the House. A contract was entered into with Messrs Hansard, and to this day the Official Report of Parliamentary Proceedings is known as 'Hansard', though Hansards have long since ceased to have anything to do with it, and since 1909 the publication has been undertaken by Her Majesty's Stationery Office.

The change was, however, gradual. Sir Robert Peel refused office in 1839 because the Queen would not show her 'confidence' in him by changing her Ladies. In 1841 it was still thought that a dissolution of Parliament was an appeal by the Queen to her people to support her Government. When the constituencies returned a Tory majority, however, and the Whigs were defeated in Parliament in consequence, the Queen sent forthwith for Sir Robert Peel,

and there was no difficulty about the Ladies. The people
had chosen and the House of Commons had voted. It mattered not what the Queen thought about Peel nor what
views the Lords might hold. The Government had to have
a majority in the Commons. In 1850 Lord John Russell's
Whig Government had specifically to face the problem. The
Lords had voted no-confidence in the Government. The
Government asked the Commons for a vote of confidence
and stayed in office when they got it. Since then the confidence or non-confidence of the Lords has been irrelevant.
In 1868, when the Conservatives were defeated at the polls,
Disraeli did not even wait for an adverse vote in the
Commons. He resigned forthwith. If the electorate had
chosen a Liberal majority in the Commons there must be a
Liberal Government. It was a waste of time to reconstruct
his Government, draft the Queen's Speech, and then be
defeated. The successive Reform Acts of 1868, 1884, 1918,
1928, and 1948 have made the position more certain. The
Government must be responsible to Parliament, but Parliament for this purpose means not the Queen in Parliament
nor the Queen, the House of Lords, and the House of Commons, but the House of Commons alone. Since the House of
Commons consists of parties supporting and opposing the
Government, the nature of the Government is determined
by the party majority, which in turn is decided (usually) by
a General Election: hence the people decide at the election
which party should take office.

Except for formal purposes, the Queen has disappeared
from Parliament completely. Queen Victoria did not fully
realize the position until 1841. She thought of the Whig
Government of 1837 to 1841 as her Government in every
sense of the term; and in her view the Tories were criticizing
not merely the Whigs, but the Queen herself. When the
electors returned Whigs they were supporting her, but when
they returned Tories they were voting against her. After
1841 this idea disappeared. If the electors supported the
Whigs (soon to be called the Liberals) she had a Whig
Government, if they supported the Tories (soon to be called
the Conservatives) she had to have a Tory Government.

She had such strong views that she could not quite keep out of the conflict between Gladstone and Disraeli, but she got herself involved behind the scenes, not in public. Since her reign there has never been any doubt that the monarch is outside politics. The Queen's assent to Bills is purely formal, for not once since Queen Anne has the formula 'Le Roy (or la Reine) s'avisera' been used. If a Bill is passed by both Houses of Parliament it becomes law as a matter of course. The policy of Her Majesty's Government may be influenced by the Queen, but in the last resort it must be a policy which is acceptable to the House of Commons.

THE HOUSE OF LORDS

The House of Lords could not withdraw from Parliament, for it is part of it, but its influence has progressively diminished. The process was inevitable because as ideas of popular government developed – even before democracy became an acceptable doctrine – the influence of the representative House inevitably rose above that of the unrepresentative House. The development might have been slower but for two factors, the odd composition of the House of Lords and the lack of political sense exhibited by some of its members. It consists of two groups: the archbishops and some of the bishops of the Church of England (excluding Wales), and the hereditary and life peers and peeresses.

The Church of England is the Established Church in England and, so long as it enjoys that favoured position, it is reasonable to associate its leaders with the process of government. On the other hand the spiritual peers have little influence in Wales, Scotland, and Ireland. Moreover, many of those enfranchised during the nineteenth century were Nonconformists, and they provided the great volume of support for the Liberal Party. The lay members of the Church of England, on the other hand, were more often Conservative than Liberal. Generally speaking the archbishops and bishops exercised their political powers with discretion, and in the present century they have rarely intervened on purely political issues; but their position was clearly anomalous. One result was that as the number of bishops increased the number of bishops' seats was not increased, and so only two archbishops, the Bishops of London, Durham, and Winchester, and the twenty-one senior bishops in order of appointment, take seats in the Lords.

For some, the very existence of a hereditary peerage may seem to be an anomaly. On the whole, though, opinion seems now to have come round to the view that titles of various kinds, including hereditary peerages, do little harm and may do some good. What is odd is not that a person is called 'lord' because his ancestor helped to get rid of the Parliament of Ireland or was one of Gladstone's obscurer supporters, but that he should sit in the House of Lords and speak and vote on matters of public policy. Of the peers of the first generation – politicians, ambassadors, governors-general, and the rest – it can generally be said that their assistance is helpful provided that they do not combine to defeat the will of the people as expressed through the House of Commons. Most of those of subsequent generations used to be spoken of as 'backwoodsmen' because they were rarely seen or heard in the House of Lords but came to vote when some proposal of great political importance was under debate.

Though in the nineteenth century most of the peerages were created by Liberal Governments, the peers were overwhelmingly Conservative, especially after the split in the Liberal Party over Home Rule in 1885. The effect was, therefore, to have a majority against the Government if it happened to be Liberal or Labour, but to have it for the Government if it was Conservative. The House was a 'revising Chamber' for Liberal or Labour measures but not for Conservative measures. The House of Lords rarely went to extremes, but Liberal and Labour Governments had often to amend their Bills in order to get them through. The question was, therefore, not whether a Second Chamber was necessary, but whether a Conservative Second Chamber was necessary.

There is something to be said for the opinion that the House of Lords should be more conservative, in the non-party sense, than the House of Commons. It is not often that a decision once taken can be reversed, and so it is wise to think twice before taking it. Any Government is capable of adopting a policy which may help it as a party in the short run but prove unfortunate to the country in the long run. Unfortunately the House of Lords was not merely conservative but Conservative, and Conservative politicians, while never wrong themselves, were not above using the strength of the House of Lords to obstruct a Liberal or Labour Government whether right or wrong. It can hardly be doubted now that Gladstone's Home Rule policy was right. In the end Conservative politicians gave Ireland far more than Home Rule. Possibly Home Rule equally would have led to an independent Irish republic, but at least that is what the opposition of the House of Lords led to. One cannot be so dogmatic about the Budget of 1909, which the peers opposed. Lloyd George's land tax was a failure, but one would like to be assured that the peers opposed it because they thought it would be a failure, and not because many of them were landowners. The main opposition was in fact directed to the beginnings of the Welfare State (the Old Age Pensions Act of 1908 and the National Insurance Act forecast for 1911) which Conservative politicians now claim, quite correctly, to be in large measure their creation.

The rejection by the peers of Lloyd George's Budget led to the diminution of the powers of the House of Lords in 1911 and the proposals to amend its composition. The powers were again cut down in 1949, and now the House can merely delay a 'Money Bill' for one month and any other public Bill (except a Bill to extend the duration of Parliament) for one year. It enables a Liberal or Labour Government (it never seriously opposes Conservative measures) to 'think again'. It has thus ceased to be a real obstruction to a parliamentary majority, but it still possesses its other – and, as some would say, more useful – powers. It can and does discuss matters of importance which are not in controversy, or matters on which all parties are agreed in principle – such as the relations with other nations of the Commonwealth, the more non-controversial aspects of foreign affairs, colonial policy, social relationships, law reform, etc. If one wants the cut and thrust of debate one must go to the Commons, but mature wisdom is often to be found in the Lords, not because the 'backwoodsmen' are wise, but because many of the first-generation peers have been experienced administrators charged with high responsibilities wherever Her Majesty's service has been carried on. On matters such as these the discussion in the Lords is often at a higher level than that in the Commons, for in the Lords nobody need make debating points.

Nor must it be forgotten that nine-tenths of even the most controversial Bill are not contentious. Once the principle is accepted to be the concern of the Commons, the Lords can very easily say: 'Why must you do this silly thing in this silly way?' It is very often possible to improve a Bill without in any way trying to obstruct its enactment: and the Commons have no time for this 'cleaning up' because they have to fight over the controversial issues. It is true that most of this 'cleaning up' is done by the Government. The experts, both inside and outside the public service, find flaws which should be replaced, and the necessary amendments are introduced in the Lords. In that process the peers play a merely formal part, but somewhere in Parliament provision must be made for this purpose.

There is, too, a good deal of committee work to be done on Private Bills and Orders, and it is often done better in the Lords than in the Commons. Most Members of Parliament are active politicians. They have been elected because they take an active part in public controversy, stand on platforms and make speeches, and attend conferences and move resolutions. They are more adept at talking generalities than in getting down to details. What is more, they like publicity, and there is no publicity to be obtained from committee work. When the House of Commons has a great deal of such work to do it is sometimes difficult to man the committees. In the Lords, on the other hand, there is a body of peers – not by any means a majority but enough for the purpose – willing to take trouble over details. About half the committee work of Parliament is done by the Lords, though, unlike Members of the Commons, the peers receive only small attendance allowances.

The truth is that parliament has to perform functions of two distinct types, though often they are intermingled. The one type involves general discussions on major issues; if those issues are controversial, the Commons are more efficient, whereas if they are not the active members of the Lords are often more efficient. The other type consists of detailed committee work on Bills, · private legislation, estimates and accounts. Financial business must be dealt with in the Commons because the Lords have no concern with finance; but in other respects the Lords give great assistance.

The result is that the old debate over the principle of a Second Chamber has almost disappeared. Whatever theoretical arguments may be advanced for or against, the fact is that the House of Lords does useful work. Now that the peers have ceased to obstruct Government measures, even the Labour Party has dropped from its programme the abolition of the House of Lords. What is wrong now – and on this the parties are agreed – is not that the Lords exist but that the House is badly composed. There have been some changes recently, not all in one direction. All the hereditary peers of Scotland, holding peerages created before 1707, may now sit, and so may hereditary peeresses. On the other hand, baronies may now be conferred as life peerages and the holders may sit; but the number of hereditary peerages created has not diminished, at least under a Conservative Government. These changes have increased the size of the House of Lords, which is now approaching one thousand. Persons holding peerages in 1963 were allowed twelve months in which to disclaim them for life, but only four did so. Persons succeeding to peerages are allowed to disclaim within twelve months, but few are likely to do so. The simple solution would be to deprive hereditary peers of their automatic right to sit, and to issue writs of summons only to those who were likely to be active in the House.

THE HOUSE OF COMMONS

The popular view that 'Parliament' and 'House of Commons' are interchangeable terms is based on political realities. The Queen has withdrawn from Parliament for all except formal purposes; the House of Lords performs useful services but they are neither spectacular nor fundamentally important; the real work of Parliament is done in the House of Commons. Its pre-eminence rests on its authority as the representative House.

The word 'representative' is susceptible of several interpretations, and the interpretation given to it in Britain depends upon certain presumptions which must be explained. In some forms of society the true representative is not elected; he may even hold his position by hereditary right. The chief of a Saxon tribe might have been the only person who could truly speak for his people, as is still the case in some parts of Africa. In India until very recently the Maharajah of a State was the father of his people, and if they had been asked to choose someone to represent them they would have chosen him as a matter of course. Some of the castes of British India and Ceylon had 'national' leaders who could speak for all members of the caste. In Germany the Nazis applied the same 'principle of leadership'. It is true that they secured power by force and fraud, but there is no evidence that the mass of the Germans disagreed with them once they were in power. The episcopal churches, especially the Roman Catholic Church, apply much the same principle, though they are able to give a theological justification. Communist countries have their own system of leadership through the Communist parties, which are based mainly on the 'industrial proletariat'.

In Britain the idea that the country should be divided into constituencies, each represented by a Member selected by ballot among all the resident adults, is quite a recent one. As its very name implies, the House of Commons was a body of people representing 'communities', the shires and the boroughs. The freemen or freeholders – the meanings were once almost identical – of the shires met together to choose two knights. In a borough the 'burgesses', who might be few or numerous, met together to choose their representatives. Nobody suggested that the common people needed to take any part in the process, for they were adequately represented by the lords, the knights, or the burgesses.

The idea of representative democracy, which is now so firmly accepted that we find it difficult to justify any other, has several sources. In the first place, it derives from Christianity, and especially from Nonconformist interpretations of Christianity. Christianity emphasized two ideas, the idea of the individual and the idea of the church. The emphasis differs according to the interpretation. Whereas the Church of England (like the Church of Rome) emphasized the idea of the church, the Nonconformists emphasized the idea of the individual: and in nineteenth-century Britain the Nonconformists led the movement for parliamentary reform. In the second place, Greek political thought, which profoundly affected European ideas after the Renaissance, brought in the theory of democracy. Greek democracy was applicable to small communities like city-states: but the idea could be hitched to the very English idea of representation, which was a product of the Norman Conquest. Thirdly, the French Revolution was based ideologically on the denial of aristocratic privilege and the affirmation of political equality. Though in the short term the Revolution caused a reaction in Britain and put back the idea of parliamentary reform, in the long term it profoundly influenced the development of ideas. For the first half of the nineteenth century the conservative ideas of Edmund Burke were dominant, but in the second half John Stuart Mill had greater influence, and his ideas are traceable through Bentham to the French Revolution.

Ideas develop in a background of economic and social change. The most important factor was the so-called Industrial Revolution. 'Revolution' is an inaccurate expression because it conveys the idea of a sudden change, whereas the process was slow and continuous for more than a hundred years. Its principal consequence was the growth of a large urban population dependent not on trade but on industry. Rural England had a stable social hierarchy, from the landless labourers to the squire and the parson. The commercial cities had a different kind of hierarchy dominated by the merchant and the craftsman. The factory worker left his rural hierarchy but did not join the commercial hierarchy. He acquired strength through his trade union and Nonconformity. In the industrial towns the only stable unit was the individual family, which could not be represented by county freeholders or urban burgesses. The agitation for the 'Charter' in the hungry forties failed immediately, but it led inevitably to the idea that the urban worker must be represented in Parliament. The Reform Act of 1867, significantly enough, enfranchised the urban householders. Meanwhile the face of rural England was changing, too. Railways and macadamized roads – the motor bus came in the present century – broke down the rural hierarchy, and the Reform Act of 1884 enfranchised the rural householder.

It must not be thought that these ideas were carefully thought out and their consequences put into legislation. Laws are made by politicians, not by political philosophers, and politicians are interested in votes. Whether Gladstone tried to reform the franchise in 1866 because he thought reform desirable, or because he thought that the Liberal Party would gain more seats, is a matter on which there might be argument. When Gladstone failed there is not much doubt about Disraeli's reason for introducing the Bill which became the Act of 1867. He thought he could 'dish the Whigs' and gain seats for the Conservatives. The fact that the Liberals won suggested that if the rural members were enfranchised in 1884 the Liberals might win again. Nevertheless, politicians adopt ideas because they are, so to speak, in the wind.

What was in the wind in 1885 was the idea of political equality. It was not argued that men were equal in social status or in ability or in education. It was not even said that the squire and the labourer were equally capable of choosing a Government. What was said was in effect that the Colonel's lady and Judy O'Grady were sisters under the skin, so that the husbands of both ought to have votes. Bentham had put it that the function of government was to achieve the greatest happiness of the greatest number. In practical politics what the philosopher says is of less importance than what the soldier says. Even so, the man in the street adopted what was in substance a utilitarian philosophy. The squire might know what was good for the squire, but only the labourer knew what was good for the labourer. Both were human beings, equal in the sight of God, with the same physical and spiritual needs; the idea of political privilege based on class – though it was not put into those terms until the elements of Marxism became known later in the century – had disappeared in the French Revolution; the only solution, therefore, was to give both the squire and the labourer a vote. Indeed it might be said – though this was a twentieth century idea – that the slum-dweller needed the vote more than the landlord because the landlord could look after himself.

The argument that the slum-dweller and the illiterate labourer were incapable of appreciating the importance of the gold standard or the reasons (if any) which justified the Boer War, was met by the answer that they were not asked to do so. They were asked to choose between two worthy gentlemen, both of whom professed to be experts in economics and colonial affairs. Edmund Burke had laid down the doctrine that he was not merely Member for Bristol but also a Member of Parliament. Though Burke lost his seat the idea gradually obtained acceptance, especially after the party organizations developed. The Member was not a delegate instructed to vote for the gold standard or against the Boer War; he was a representative chosen to decide these issues because he was the more acceptable candidate.

In fact, though, the man in the street did not attempt to work out a philosophy of democratic government. He thought he was as much entitled to the vote as the boss. That was a good and sufficient reason for adult suffrage, though a century was needed to bring it about. It is not the

British practice to adopt a principle and forthwith to carry it to its logical conclusion. First the urban householder was enfranchised, then the rural householder, then the lodger and then all the adult males. It was left to the twentieth century, after a fierce controversy, to enfranchise the women; and the change was effected in two stages – women over thirty in 1918 and women under thirty in 1928. Even then the idea of political equality was not completely carried out. If the Colonel's lady and Judy O'Grady were sisters under the skin each ought to have one vote: but until 1948 some people had two votes, though in different constituencies.

Moreover, the idea of political equality necessarily implied that each vote should have the same value. If Bath and Bristol, Lancashire and Rutlandshire, each had two seats, the votes were obviously of unequal value. If there were four times as many electors in Bristol as there were in Bath, each vote in Bath was worth four times as much as a vote in Bristol. The idea of the representation of communities had therefore to disappear. The larger counties and boroughs had to be divided into single-member constituencies. This process was begun in 1885 but it was not completed until 1948. Since then the principle of 'one man (or woman), one vote, one value' has been carried out almost (though not completely) logically.

The danger of purely armchair speculation on political matters is shown by the fact that John Stuart Mill, whose *Representative Government*, published in 1861, was the most thorough exposition of representative democracy, did not even mention parties. The explanation is that the party system as we know it grew out of the extension of the franchise and that Mill had not foreseen what sterner realists like Disraeli saw very quickly. In the small and more or less homogeneous electorates of the first half of the nineteenth century the candidate's principal claim to election was the support of influential backers. Owing to the static and hierarchic nature of rural society, a large proportion of the electors would vote for the nominee of a great landowner like the Duke of Bedford, the Earl of Derby, or the Earl of

Lonsdale. The parliamentary handbooks described many of the constituencies as within the 'influence' of this or that great landowner. There were other constituencies where the electorate was larger, where nobody had much 'influence' and where, therefore, the corrupt methods caricatured in Dickens' story of the election at Eatanswill were frequently used. As the electorate grew larger, 'influence' declined and corruption became more difficult and expensive. On what basis could a comparatively insignificant person like the average parliamentary candidate appeal to the free and independent electors of a large constituency? Even the 'influence' of the Earl of Derby could not extend to the population of Manchester. Bribery and corruption were not only met by more stringent laws but also became so expensive that it was not worth while to seek the glory of election to Parliament. The only basis on which a person could appeal to so large and varied an electorate was that he was a good party man pledged to support Disraeli or Gladstone.

There were parties in the eighteenth century, but they were groups of political 'friends' in Parliament. Those who were elected through the 'influence' of a great Whig lord were obviously Whigs. The relationship was, however, in large measure personal. If the great lord did not get the Garter when he thought he ought, or if his youngest son was not given the colonial appointment which his qualities merited, there was a split in the Whigs and the prospects of the Tories were improved. Sir Robert Peel was the first to realize after 1832 that something more than the 'management' of members and their backers was required to secure a majority. He himself appealed to the electors of Tamworth in 1834, and through them to electors generally, on the basis of a party policy. What is more, he began the practice of establishing local organizations. In those days registration was not automatic, but a person qualified to exercise the vote had to make good his claim. To secure a Conservative majority, therefore, it was necessary to ensure that enough Conservative supporters were on the electoral registers, and this could be done only in the constituencies themselves. When Disraeli failed to 'dish the Whigs' in 1868 he realized that a stronger local organization was needed in the towns, in which the householders had been enfranchised by the Reform Act of 1867. It was, however, Joseph Chamberlain who showed in Birmingham what efficient party organization could do; and, though there were criticisms of this 'caucus' system, the Liberal Party as a whole and the Conservative Party paid him the compliment of copying his methods.

The result of these developments was to alter democratic theory. The electors of West Birmingham did not look around to see who was the most suitable candidate to represent their views and interests in Parliament. There was a self-constituted Liberal Association to seek a candidate pledged to support Gladstone, and a self-constituted Conservative Association to find a candidate pledged to support Disraeli. Few of the electors knew anything about Doe or Roe, but they knew about Gladstone and Disraeli. If Doe supported Gladstone and Roe supported Disraeli, the average elector knew which way to cast his vote.

It was of course possible for Mr Blank to stand as a candidate without a 'label' or with a 'label' of his own; but very few electors would know Mr Blank, and his 'label' did not help as much as the label 'Conservative' or 'Liberal'. All over the country the real battle was between the Liberals and the Conservatives, and only occasionally could an independent or a member of a small party slip in. It was this development which enabled Burke's doctrine to be carried out. If Doe was elected his main job was not to forward the interests of the people of West Birmingham but to support the policy of the Liberal Parliamentary Party. Naturally he had to consider the interests and prejudices of his own constituents, but in the process he must not prejudice the prospects of the Liberal Party in other constituencies. Privileges could not be given to West Birmingham unless they were also given elsewhere. The national interest predominated because the parties were national organizations. Sectional interests could be supported only if they were large sections. Since the Liberal Party had the support of the great mass of Nonconformists its policy was necessarily influenced by Nonconformist sentiment. Since 'The Trade' was usually Conservative the Conservatives were not keen on the Nonconformist policy of restricting the sale of liquor. There were, however, limits beyond which sectional interests could not be supported. Though most of the county members wanted a tax on imported corn which would 'maintain British agriculture', as some would put it, or 'increase landlords' incomes', as others would put it, the Conservative Party as a whole could not adopt such a policy without having the support of the urban workers.

In the course of the present century the Labour Party has succeeded the Liberal Party as the main opposition to the Conservatives, but the principle remains the same. The real question submitted to the electors is whether there shall be a Conservative Government or a Labour Government. So plain was the situation as early as 1868 that when the Liberals obtained a majority Disraeli resigned forthwith, not waiting to be defeated in Parliament. The precedent has been followed since.

The party conflict dominates the House of Commons. The House consists in effect of two parts, the party in office and the party out of office. Even the seating arrangements make this plain. The Government party sits to the right of Mr Speaker and the Opposition party to the left. The party leaders sit in the 'front benches', with the clerks' table between them. They address Mr Speaker, but they speak at each other across the table. If a member changes party he is said to 'cross the floor'. There may be smaller groups and even a few 'independent' members pledged to neither party, but in the main, for reasons already given, the elector chooses between the candidates of the major parties. He knows that his task is to choose which party shall form the Government, and normally he votes for the one or the other.

The characteristic of the British Constitution – it was invented in Britain – is that the Government is in Parliament. When the British Constitution was studied by Frenchmen in the eighteenth century this was not the characteristic which they emphasized. On the contrary, the King was then the real head of the Government and he chose his Ministers as he pleased. It is true that he or his Ministers had to secure a majority in the House of Commons in order to get his money votes through, but there were always members who would support the King, and if he had the support of one of the larger groups of peers also, who influenced the votes in the Commons, he could generally secure a majority. Even as late as 1783 George III could dismiss the Fox-North Coalition and ask a young man named William Pitt to form a Ministry. Nor was the Ministry necessarily a party Ministry. Ministers usually wanted to serve with their political 'friends', but it was not impossible for individuals or groups to continue from one Ministry to another. What impressed the French commentators was not that the King's Government controlled Parliament, but that Parliament was independent of the King. They thought that the liberty of the people of Britain – which was a remarkable phenomenon before the French Revolution – depended on the fact that, while the King governed, he had to govern according to law, that the law could be changed only in an independent Parliament, and that the interpretation of the laws was left to judges who, though appointed by the King, were secured in an independent position by the Act of Settlement. In most parts of Europe powers were concentrated in the King, which produced tyranny; but in Britain there was a separation of powers into three groups, which produced the familiar British liberty.

The American colonists were impressed by these arguments. Indeed, they thought that the essential defect of the British Constitution, which had compelled them to rebel against the King, was that the King interfered too much in Parliament by appointing Members of Parliament to public offices and so depriving Parliament of its independence. The Constitution of the United States – leaving aside its federal aspect, necessitated by the union of thirteen independent States – is therefore based on the British Constitution as the Americans thought it ought to work. A President elected by an electoral college replaces George III, the

Congress consists of two Houses elected by the people of the States, the judges of the Supreme Court were made independent, and the President's Ministers (or Secretaries) were forbidden to sit in the Congress.

The British Constitution developed by a different road. George III appointed William Pitt in 1783, but Pitt appealed to the electorate. The King helped him to get a majority, but Pitt's authority rested as much on that majority as on the support of the King. Though the King could still influence policy and even change his Ministers, during the next forty years there was a gradual transfer of power – much assisted in the early years by the King's periodical fits of insanity – from the King to the Ministers. Though Queen Victoria did not realize it until 1841, executive authority rested not in the monarch but in the Government selected from the majority party in the House of Commons. In 1841 Peel's authority rested not on the Queen – except in a purely formal sense – but on the Tory majority elected at the general election. The head of the Government was not the Queen but the Queen's chief or Prime Minister. He chose his colleagues from his party supporters in Parliament, and so long as he kept his majority he remained in office. When he lost his majority in 1846 he promptly resigned.

Nothing in the law requires the Prime Minister to be a Member of the House of Commons. During the 130 years since the Reform Act of 1832 there have been eight Prime Ministers in the House of Lords. The last of them was the Marquess of Salisbury, who held office for the third time from 1895 to 1902. On the resignation of Bonar Law in 1923 a peer, Lord Curzon, was the obvious candidate but he was passed over by George V in favour of a commoner, Baldwin. The reason was that the rise of the Labour Party had centred the party conflict in the House of Commons. Probably, though, the rise of the Labour Party had merely accentuated an inevitable development. Though it has gained in other respects, the House of Lords has lost ground as a centre of political interest. There have been exceptions, but during the past fifty years few of the more important

Ministers have been peers; and during the two recent periods when the Foreign Secretary was in the House of Lords there were protests against the arrangement, even though the Prime Minister himself undertook to answer Foreign Office questions in the House of Commons.

Essentially, therefore, the Government consists of persons chosen from among the majority in the House of Commons. It is faced by an alternative Government which hopes to come into office at the next election. On the one side is the Prime Minister, on the other the Leader of the Opposition; on the one side is the Secretary of State for Foreign Affairs, on the other an Opposition member who has been, or hopes to be, Foreign Secretary and pays special attention to foreign policy; on the one side is the Minister of Education and on the other the 'shadow' Minister of Education. The debate ebbs and flows across the floor.

This party conflict, which at first sight seems rather odd, is simply an unusually logical application (for Britain) of fundamental principles. The basic assumption is that in matters of politics – and politics may extend even to religion – opinions may properly differ. It is rarely possible to say that one line of development is right and the other wrong. There is a choice of alternatives, and no honest man can guarantee that he will choose the better. What he can do is to marshal the arguments, reach a conclusion, and ask others if they do not agree with him. He will admit that another might marshal the arguments differently and reach a different conclusion. Indeed, anybody who has sat on committees knows that opinion develops in the course of discussion. One starts with a tentative conclusion and ends with a different one. Discussion would be useless if it were not so. At the end of the discussion, though, there may still be disagreement even about such a matter as the drainage of the tennis court, and the only solution is to take a vote.

The free citizens of a Greek city could meet together and decide matters like a large committee: the thirty million adult citizens of the United Kingdom cannot. There are three ways of meeting the problem. The first is to select an emperor or a dictator and let Caesar decide, a process which leads ultimately, as Mussolini saw, to the conclusion that Caesar is always right. The second is to select a theory of government like free enterprise or communism and let those who support that theory decide, a process which, as the Soviet Union has demonstrated, leads to the conclusion that the party is always right and cannot allow any other theory to be held or even any variation in the application of the theory. The third is the British method – or perhaps it should be called the English method because it was invented in England – of electing persons of different shades of opinion and letting them decide, at least for a short period.

In matters of no great importance like the time of opening of the public baths or the provision of a children's room at the public library, it is possible to start the discussion with an open mind and reach a sensible conclusion. Matters of ·greater moment depend upon one's line of approach, or upon the ultimate objective that one is seeking to achieve, or upon the methodology of achieving the objective. The representatives therefore tend to coalesce into parties. For the purposes of election it is desirable that they should, for one cannot agree that the decision be taken by Tom, Dick, and Harry unless one knows the attitude which they adopt to questions of principle. It does not follow that there need be two parties only, but the machine works more easily if there are. One party thus takes the decisions under a fire of criticism from the other. The Government decides and the Opposition criticizes, both appealing to the opinion of the people whom they represent.

The Opposition is thus an essential part of the House of Commons. The assertion made by Sir William Harcourt that 'the function of an Opposition is to oppose' is not wholly correct. Many proposals of the Government are not opposed because there is general agreement. Incidental details may be criticized or even opposed, for a scheme which is good in principle may be weak in its details. It is possible, too, to criticize a proposal without opposing it. The Opposition may agree that increased armaments are necessary, but assert that the reason for the necessity is the unfortunate foreign policy of the Government. If a scheme is opposed, it does not follow that every part of it must be opposed. Finally, opposition is usually formal. The Opposition's task is not to prevent the Government from carrying out its policy but to criticize that policy in the hope that the electors will choose a different Government next time. The Queen's service must be carried on, and so long as a party is in power it must be carried on by that party. Hence there is nothing hypocritical in agreeing with the Government that opposition be kept up until 10 p.m. to-morrow night and that a vote then be taken. The Government's policy has been adequately criticized but not obstructed, and the Queen's service can be carried on. If there are proposals about which the Opposition feels so strongly that it must obstruct, the Government has to use its powers – which are ample – to overcome the obstruction, for the Queen's service must be carried on. Frequent use of these powers has harmful effects. It gives rise to the idea that the way to deal with an Opposition is to vote it down. It is easier for a Government to stop criticism than to answer it, for then the electors know only one side of the case. If the Opposition constantly obstructed and the Government consistently voted it down the dictatorship of the majority would soon be established.

Once these principles are understood the scheme falls into place. The Government governs under criticism from the Opposition. The Opposition's functions are almost as important as those of the Government. Its Leader is paid a salary and accommodation is provided for the Opposition whips. So far as possible proceedings are regulated by agreement between Government and Opposition. If there is disagreement the Government must decide and use its majority for the purpose; but since the Opposition agrees that the Government must govern and the Government agrees that the Opposition must criticize, the order of proceedings can usually be settled in conference.

Since the House consists of two sets of politicians, it functions best when it debates political issues of some magnitude. Though it has also to do a good deal of com-

mittee work, politicians are usually elected not because
they are good administrators or committee men, but because
they can make attractive and plausible speeches – though
there are certainly many exceptions. What is more, these
general political debates are the only part of the work of the
House which receives adequate publicity. Technical details
cannot be popularized; nor indeed are there many electors
interested in them. The real purpose of parliamentary
debate is to bring home to the electorate the major conflicts
of policy. One of the problems of government is to enable
this to be done. The Official Report, commonly called
Hansard, is read by few. Nor indeed is it convenient to read,
because it has to record every word of every speech, though
much of what is said is of no particular importance and can
be read only by those with much leisure and more patience.
The newspaper technique of selection is essential. Unfortunately space in newspapers is limited, and they have to give
their readers what they want, not what they ought to want.
The fact that the average reader is 'not interested in
politics' is by no means a trait to be deplored. If it were an
indication of a scale of values in which a poet was considered
more worthy than a politician it would be a positive merit.
Even when it is purely negative, though, it shows that
Britain's political problems are not acute and that her
government is, on the whole, well-managed. When the
elector has to choose a new Government, after four or five
years, however, he must find it difficult to do his duty
conscientiously if he has read nothing of parliamentary
proceedings except the occasional 'scene', as the sub-
editors call it.

In spite of this difficulty the House of Commons does its
job well. It does it better, for instance, than the House of
Representatives in the United States. The reason is plain:
it is because both the Government and the Opposition are
in Parliament. The Prime Minister does not need to have
a weekly press conference, like the President of the United
States. During the parliamentary session he and his
Ministers have a press conference five days a week. Questions are asked not by pressmen anxious for a 'story' but by

skilled politicians, many of whom have experience in office. If a subject is important, the case for the Government is stated at length and is followed by the case for the Opposition, stated at equal length. The argument passes to and fro across the floor until the subject, the audience, or the time is exhausted. It is the finest press conference in the world.

The proceedings of the House are organized for this purpose. On every day except Friday proceedings open – after formalities – with 'questions'. There may be fifty or more such questions, some important, some not, to which Ministers give prepared answers. If the subject-matter is interesting, members ask supplementary questions arising out of the answer, and the Minister has to answer without a brief unless his official advisers have foreseen the 'supplementaries'. This process lasts three-quarters of an hour, and then comes the business of the day. Sometimes private members take the floor because they have been given time to move motions or recommend Bills. Most of the time of the House, though, is taken up with Government business based on motions or Bills introduced by Ministers. This is the opportunity for the Opposition to criticize the Government's policy and for the Government to defend it. If the motion is for the second reading of a National Health Bill, the Government's policy in relation to the National Health Scheme is debated; if the motion is to vote £75,000,000 for the Ministry of Education, the Government's educational policy is debated. Indeed, the motions to be put down are, so far as may be possible, settled weekly by discussions between the whips, so that the Government may defend its policy and the Opposition criticize it. If the Government wishes to secure the enactment of legislation or a vote of funds, and the Opposition sees no objection and no means of making political capital, it goes through without debate. The House of Commons is part of a law-making machine and it is in charge of the national finances, but it spends the great majority of its time in political debate. The inhabitants of Fiji or the Seychelles may complain that the Mother of Parliaments gives little time to their affairs; but it never will give much time until the Government does something that the Opposition wishes to criticize. The colony whose affairs are never debated is, comparatively speaking, a happy place, because it is being governed without political controversy.

It sometimes happens that controversy arises suddenly, after the programme for the week has been compiled. The Standing Orders provide for such a contingency. If a Member moves the adjournment of the House to discuss 'a definite matter of urgent public importance', if Mr Speaker agrees that the question falls within that definition, and if forty Members rise in their places to support the motion, the subject is debated the same evening. Messengers rush off to Whitehall to get the files and prepare a brief for the Minister. If the problem arose in Belfast or Basutoland the telephone and the telegraph are set to work. The Government is being criticized within a few hours; its defence must be hurriedly prepared.

It must not be thought that the subject of debate is always a national or international problem affecting millions of people or millions of pounds. The House of Commons prides itself on being the protector of the liberty of the subject. John Hampden has a whole chapter in our history because he refused to pay twenty shillings. A woman found in Hyde Park in what the police believed to be a compromising situation was responsible for a debate, a Commission of Inquiry and a Royal Commission because some considered the procedure of the police to be unconscionable. A British subject from Malta who believed himself badly treated by a foreign Government nearly brought about the fall of the Government of the United Kingdom and certainly produced one of Lord Palmerston's most famous speeches. Such occasions are rare because the need for them is fortunately rare: but the official who begins to 'push around' some obscure citizen or other runs the risk of a debate in Parliament in which somebody will quote Magna Carta, 'nec super eum ibimus'. That may not be what King John understood by the phrase, but it fulfils its purpose. The mere existence of the House of Commons containing both Government and

Opposition compels the official, high or low, to be wary how he treads, for he may spring a mine whose explosion reverberates around the world. There can be no concentration camps in Britain unless their need is defended and approved in Parliament. As Magna Carta put it: 'Nullus liber homo capiatur vel imprisonetur ... nisi per legale judicium parium suorum, vel per legem terre'. Not only may the 'liber homo' appeal to the Courts, he may also appeal to Parliament and thence to the people.

This parliamentary control is admirable when it relates to the liberty of the subject; it has defects when it relates to the ordinary process of government. A public servant works under a constant fear of parliamentary criticism, not of himself directly but of his Minister. Much time is spent in preparing answers to questions and briefs for public speeches. Action must be recorded in writing so that its consequences may be justified. The formalities must be observed because, if anything goes wrong, Parliament may criticize; though Parliament is equally critical of the 'red tape' which adherence to formalities requires. In financial matters in particular detailed rules have to be followed meticulously because, if there is some defalcation, not merely the official concerned but also his superior officers may be involved if they have not observed the rules in detail. Parliamentary criticism therefore makes public administration formal and dilatory, unsuited, for instance, for the operation of commercial and industrial enterprises.

Though emphasis must be given to the function of the House of Commons as the forum for political debate, it also has less spectacular functions to perform. It is part of the legislature, and British legislation is lengthy and detailed. Many legislatures are content to lay down general principles and to authorize their working out in detail by administrative decrees. Parliament and the people of Britain have derived from their conflicts with the Stuarts a suspicion against legislation by decree. It is true that, as legislation has grown, both in size and in complexity, Parliament has had to delegate powers of legislation by statutory instruments. Nevertheless, there is no general constitutional power for this purpose. Specific powers are given for specific purposes and are closely defined. A Bill may therefore be a hundred pages or two hundred pages long, every word of which has to be specifically approved by Parliament.

Normally a Bill is 'read a first time' by reading its long title. There is no debate, and the House authorizes it to be printed. Its principles are debated on second reading. It is then referred to a Standing Committee where it is examined in detail. It is divided into clauses, each of which is put separately as a motion, 'That clause . . . stand part of the Bill.' Members may, and often do, move amendments. When these amendments have been disposed of, the clause itself is voted upon. This process may take weeks. When the Bill has been approved in committee, it is reported to the House, and further amendments may then be proposed, though on the report stage the clauses are not put separately unless they are amended. Finally, the general principles of the Bill as amended are discussed on the third reading. If there are financial clauses in the Bill, and most Bills have such clauses, there will be two extra stages, either before or after the second reading. A financial resolution is moved and debated in the Committee of the Whole House (the House without the Speaker) and reported to the House itself.

The House also exercises, so far as it can, detailed control of public finance. The composition and procedure of the House are not well adapted for this purpose, and the debates in which, theoretically, it examines the estimates of public expenditure have in fact become debates on the various policies for which funds have to be provided. Every year, though, a group of estimates is examined in detail by a Select Committee. Further, the audited accounts, with the reports of the Comptroller and Auditor-General on them, are examined annually by the Public Accounts Committee. The Comptroller and Auditor-General is an independent official, not under ministerial control, who authorizes the issue of public funds in accordance with the votes passed by Parliament and audits the accounts to ascertain that the money has been spent in accordance with the rules and for the objects specified by Parliament. He reports direct to the

House of Commons, and the Public Accounts Committee examines in detail any criticism that they may have to offer.

Nor must it be forgotten that, in the Commons or in the Lords, there is a great deal of committee work to be done on private Bills and statutory orders. It is not always easy to find enough members to serve on all these committees, nor to find time for committee discussions without trenching upon the time of the House itself.

THE TRANSFER OF POWER

THE formula 'Her Majesty's Government' is not a legal term. On the few occasions on which 'the Government of the United Kingdom' or some similar phrase has been used in legal documents the Courts have had some difficulty in finding out exactly what it was intended to mean. In principle, the powers of government are vested in the Queen. She sends and receives diplomatic representatives, communicates with other Heads of States, enters into treaties, declares war and makes peace, commands the Royal Navy, the Army, and the Royal Air Force, appoints Governors-General and Governors to administer her dominions beyond the seas, controls foreign trade, issues currency, carries the mails, and exercises many other functions which it would be difficult to list. She cannot enact legislation except by and with the advice and consent of the Lords Spiritual and Temporal, and Commons, in Parliament assembled. Nor can she impose taxation except by authority of an Act of Parliament.

Even in a legal sense, though, the situation has altered in the last century. Generally speaking the new functions of government, which the State has assumed in consequence of the growth of democratic ideas, are exercised under legal powers vested by Parliament not in the monarch but in Ministers. Thus, powers relating to education are vested not in the Queen but in the Minister of Education. Though the roads are the Queen's highways and in a legal sense the surfaces of the roads are vested in her, powers over the roads are vested in the Minister of Transport. Similarly, powers relating to local government, housing, town and country planning, labour, agriculture, etc., are vested in the appropriate Ministers. Even where some legal powers are vested in the Queen, it will generally be found that the greater part of the powers of government is vested not in her but in the Secretary of State, the Lords Commissioners of the

Admiralty, the Army Council, The Air Council, the Lords Commissioners of the Treasury, the Lord Chancellor, the Board of Trade, or the Postmaster-General, as the case may be. All these persons and bodies act on behalf of the Queen in the sense that they are appointed by her, their employees are her servants, the property which they hold is the Queen's property, and the contracts into which they enter are contracts on behalf of the Crown. Nevertheless, the powers are not her powers. When, for instance, a formal notification is conveyed by an Assistant Secretary that a town and country planning scheme has been approved, he does not say 'I am commanded by Her Majesty —' but 'I am directed by the Minister —'. The Assistant Secretary takes the decision not in the name of the Queen but in the name of his Minister, because the legal power is vested by Act of Parliament in the Minister.

This does not mean that all the older powers are vested in the Queen and all the newer powers are vested in Ministers. Generally speaking, if an older power was not of great importance it has been superseded by more modern legislation, while if a new power is of special constitutional importance it is vested in the Queen. For instance, though the Royal Air Force is a modern creation, it has been assimilated to the Army, so that the command is vested in the Queen and a direct connexion between the Queen and the officers and airmen has been created. Even when a colony is governed under statutory authority, its Constitution is in Letters Patent issued by the Queen or in an Order of the Queen in Council. During the last war, emergency powers were exercised under an Act of Parliament which authorized the King in Council to issue Orders, but those Orders authorized various Ministers to issue Regulations. The provisions of greater constitutional importance were in Orders in Council and those of less importance in Regulations.

Statements such as 'The Queen is the executive' should therefore be discounted. Until the eighteenth century the monarch really governed the country though, unlike his foreign contemporaries, he had to govern under the law, which could be altered only in Parliament. Either the law or political pressure – it was never very clear which – compelled the medieval king to consult his Council, which consisted of such officials as the Chancellor and the Treasurer and such great lords as he chose to summon. The recurrent disputes between the kings and the barons were caused by, or at least led to complaints about, the failure of the kings to consult the right people. Owing to the disappearance of the barons in the fifteenth century and the absolutist tendencies of the first two Stuarts the Council became a mere royal instrument; and under Charles I, especially in the form of the Court of Star Chamber and the Court of High Commission, it was regarded as an instrument of royal oppression. Its judicial powers (except in respect of matters arising in the courts overseas) were, however, abolished by the Long Parliament in 1641. Under Charles II an attempt was made to revive the Council as a consultative body, but these attempts failed because the King disliked discussing his affairs with 'a set of fellows', and preferred to settle matters privately with the principal officials in his ante-chamber or 'cabinet'.

After the Hanoverian Succession this 'Cabinet' became a more important body. George I and George II were still Electors of Hanover and were more concerned with the complicated disputes of Germany than with the affairs of their kingdom of Great Britain. George I, too, knew no English, found it a bore to attend discussions which he could not follow, and so meetings of the principal officials in Cabinet were usually held in his absence. The Hanoverians succeeded under a purely parliamentary title laid down in the Act of Settlement, 1701. There was a Stuart, or at least an alleged Stuart, ready to sit on the throne if the Hanoverians were turned out – and there were rebellions in 1715 and 1745. Nor had the King power to repel the Pretender unless Parliament passed the Mutiny Act every year, for the Act of Settlement forbade a standing army in time of peace. Finally, the cost of government simply could not be met unless Parliament was prepared to make regular grants.

It followed that the first two Georges had to govern through Ministers who could persuade Parliament to be reasonable. Generally speaking they had to be Whigs, for the loyalty of the Tories was doubted so long as there was a Stuart Pretender. Besides, the Whigs predominated among the great landowners whose 'influence' was important in elections to the House of Commons. These Whigs would normally support the King because they were mainly responsible for putting George I on the throne, and their condition would not be happy if the Stuarts were restored. Even so, both they and the members of the Commons had to be 'managed'. The 'management' was done mainly through the Treasury, whose functions were controlled by Lords Commissioners. The First Lord of the Treasury thus became principal adviser to the King or Prime Minister. Sir Robert Walpole, who was First Lord from 1721 to 1742, repudiated the term, but he was in effect the first Prime Minister.

George III had none of the inhibitions of George I and George II and more anxiety to be a real king. Even he had to govern with a majority and for twenty years he found pliant instruments. After the appointment of William Pitt in 1783, though, effective power passed more and more into the hands of the Prime Minister and the Cabinet. Though there were a few relics of old traditions when Victoria became Queen in 1837, the responsibility really rested not in the Queen but in 'Her Majesty's Government'.

The 'Ministers' who exercised the powers of the Queen were the successors of those royal servants who really had ministered to, or at least advised, her predecessors. The Treasurer had been replaced by Lords Commissioners, of whom the First Lord was in the Cabinet, while the Chancellor of the Exchequer had ceased to be a clerk and had become a leading Minister. The Chancellor had become the Lord Chancellor, while the privy or private seal had become vested in a Lord Privy Seal. The King's secretary had become a Secretary of State and the office had multiplied. The Admiralty had been put into commission and was represented in the Cabinet by the First Lord. The Board of Trade, which had begun as a committee of the Council, was represented by the President of the Board. The Duchy of

Lancaster, which had never been completely fused with the Crown, was represented by its Chancellor. The Commissioners for Works and Public Buildings were represented by the First Commissioner.

There is nothing in the law to compel the Queen to delegate her functions to these Ministers. Though it is true that 'the Queen never acts alone', it is not at all certain that the law requires the concurrence of a Minister. There was, for instance, nothing to stop the King of England from making a secret agreement with the French King, unknown to the Secretary of State.* Possibly the Secretary of State would have resigned, and in the nineteenth century not only he but the whole Ministry would have resigned. That, no doubt, is the key to the whole arrangement. The monarch was dependent on Parliament and therefore was compelled by the force of political circumstances to employ Ministers who could manage Parliament. In the eighteenth century this gave him a fairly wide choice, though even George III was compelled to employ the Earl of Chatham and, later, to accept the Fox-North Coalition. A Minister's security of tenure therefore depended both upon the 'confidence' or support of the King and the 'confidence' or support of Parliament. Many factors combined, in the fifty years between the dismissal of the Fox-North Coalition in 1783 and the Reform Act of 1832, to strengthen the power of Parliament and to weaken the power of the King. Hence the Ministers relied more and more on the 'confidence' of Parliament but less and less on the 'confidence' of the King. The King had to depend on his Ministers because they had ceased to depend upon him.

It was never assumed in the eighteenth century that a Government had to be politically homogeneous. William III had to rely mainly on the Whigs because they had been primarily responsible for the Revolution Settlement under which he held the Crown. Anne relied mainly on the Tories because she preferred them. George I and George II relied mainly on the Whigs because the loyalty of many of the

* It could not be a treaty, because that required the use of the Great Seal, which the Lord Chancellor kept.

Tories was suspect. George III tried to rely on his own strength and, with Lord North's compliance, he succeeded for nearly twenty years. If, however, the Prime Minister insisted that the offices be distributed among his political 'friends' the King had either to agree or to find a new Prime Minister. If the 'friends' stuck together and could control a majority in Parliament the King had Hobson's choice. Usually, though, that situation did not arise. The Whigs and the Tories were not fast, disciplined parties like the parties of today. They were in groups depending on the political strength of a particular leader. Thus, the Rockingham Whigs joined with the Tories after the French Revolution, the Reform Act was made possible by the junction of the Canningite Tories with the Foxite Whigs; and so on. Until the parties themselves became strong, especially after the Reform Act, the King could play off one group against another. In any case he could usually insist that a particular friend of his, like Lord Thurlow under George III, remain in office no matter who was Prime Minister.

Homogeneity and collective responsibility go together. The King could be prevented from playing off one group against another if the Ministers presented what the modern communists would call a 'united front'. If they held a majority and if they stuck together the King was bound to keep them in office. Collective responsibility was originally collective responsibility towards the King, but its value depended on the support of a parliamentary majority. As the importance of the King's 'confidence' diminished, collective responsibility meant that the Government was collectively responsible to the House of Commons.

All these tendencies were strengthened after the Reform Act because the extension of the franchise and the extinction of 'rotten boroughs' made the House of Commons less dependent on the great landowners and more dependent on the urban middle class. Little political support could be obtained by giving the Garter to a duke, an earldom to a baron, a baronetcy to a squire, or the Bath to a scion of a noble house. The use of 'offices of profit' and pensions had been diminished by Burke's Economy Act of 1782, and there was a gradual extinction of corrupt methods under Pitt and his successors. Though George III gave great help to Pitt in acquiring a majority in 1783, William IV could not assist the Whigs and Canningite Tories in 1832. The Government therefore ceased to be dependent upon the King and became dependent upon the electorate. When Queen Victoria came to the throne in 1837 she inherited considerable power of advising, warning and bringing pressure to bear on her Ministers, but actual power of government was vested in 'Her Majesty's Government'.

AGENCIES OF GOVERNMENT

Concentration on 'politics' causes us to over-emphasize the part played by the central administrative machine and the part played in that machine by the politicians. Because of the wisdom and efficiency of the Norman and Angevin kings, England became the first of the nation-States, with a strong central bureaucracy. There were no local potentates to compete with the King. The King's peace extended throughout England and, after Edward I, into Wales. The King's writ ran everywhere. This result was obtained, however, not by concentrating authority in the King's own hand, but by co-ordinating and systematizing the strong local organization of the Anglo-Saxons under the control of Norman central institutions. The shires became counties, but they were governed not by counts but by the freeholders meeting in the county court (shire moot) under the eye of the King's representative, the shire reeve or sheriff and under the control of the King's own court. From the fourteenth century they were governed even more efficiently (considering the general inefficiency of medieval government) by local men commissioned by the King as justices of the peace. These justices continued to govern the counties until they were superseded, for administrative purposes, by the county councils in 1889.

The towns did not become 'free cities' independent of royal authority, like so many of the towns of Germany and Holland, but they had 'liberties' under their charters involving greater or less freedom from the organization of the counties to which they belonged. Most of them had their own courts, some had separate commissions of the peace, a few even elected their own sheriffs, and all of them had councils selected by the 'freemen' of the town. Even the City of London, the most independent and powerful of them all, was subject to the King's jurisdiction.

It was this combination of local autonomy and central control which made the English system of government so remarkably efficient in a world in which the break-up of the Roman Empire and the establishment of the feudal system led to a chaos of competing jurisdictions and warring local potentates. To this day the tradition remains. Though modern methods of communication have made efficient government by a central bureaucracy much easier, and though there is a growing tendency for the Central Government to take over functions from the local authorities, the three countries of the United Kingdom, but more especially England and Wales, are still outstanding because of the strength of their local institutions. The Lancashire County Council or the Birmingham City Council does not regard itself as an instrument of Her Majesty's Government. It is governed under Acts of Parliament, it receives financial assistance from the Central Government, and often its proposals need the approval of Ministers, but it is an authority in its own right, running its affairs in its own way, and regarded by everybody as an autonomous body. We have a Ministry of Education, but it provides no schools. Certain schools receive grants direct from the Ministry, but in the main the schools are provided or assisted by the local education authorities.

This tradition of the autonomous authority operating under royal charter or commission or Act of Parliament was obviously capable of extension. Among the ancient corporations which survive to this day are the Universities of Oxford and Cambridge and the Inns of Court. Their autonomy has been extended by charter or Act of Parliament to other universities and professional organizations. When the practice of agriculture changed under the Tudors, co-operative action for land drainage became necessary and Commissioners of Sewers were appointed. As the Industrial Revolution changed the face of England, this precedent in turn was followed by the establishment of a vast network of statutory authorities, such as the turnpike trustees, the railway and canal companies, the water and drainage boards, the harbour authorities, and the gas and electricity companies. It is essential to emphasize this 'gas and water socialism', for it supplied the precedent for the modern statutory corporation. There are exceptions like the Post Office, which operates the postal, telegraphic, and telephonic system, but they are exceptions. Generally speaking a public service is provided not by a Government Department but by a public corporation like the B.B.C., the British Railways Commission, or the Electricity Council. Even public assistance is provided by a statutory body, the National Assistance Board.

To speak of these local authorities, chartered corporations and statutory boards and commissions as exercising 'delegated power' is inaccurate. The powers were not conferred on some central authority and then delegated. The principle of decentralization has always been accepted because, until recently, the central administration of services under Ministerial control was thought to be neither practicable nor desirable. Britain has been a country in which even 'decentralization' is an inaccurate term, because there never was centralization. The idea that Ministers must control everything is a recent development, about whose desirability there may be argument. It arises from the belief, which has never been adequately justified, that the life of a vast community of fifty million people can be 'planned' by a group of politicians sitting in Cabinet and assisted by a great array of administrators and technical experts. One of the problems of the modern State is to provide an organization capable of exercising the numerous functions which the State has taken upon itself: and it may be that the tradition of leaving the parish to look after the parish pump, a tradition which arose because the pump was too far from Whitehall, supplies the answer. If nobody can pump water until he has a licence from Whitehall, there will probably be more paper than water and more officials than consumers.

Nor should it be assumed that the parish pump is unimportant. If we regard the citizen as a person in his own right and not as an anonymous unit of a nation or a class – if in other words we forget Hegel and Marx – his immediate environment is as important to him as the affairs of the nation. The multiplication of population since the Industrial Revolution and its collection in large towns, the inevitable provision of services on a large scale, the use of methods of mass production in industry, and, in short, the mechanized State, have given rise to the idea, rarely precisely formulated, that the State is an end in itself. In the last analysis the State consists of John Smith, his wife and children, and their children. As every John Smith knows, a drink of water at bedtime may cause more rumpus than the expropriation of an oil company or a war in the Congo. Excessive concentration on one's private affairs and lack of attention to national and international affairs are to be deprecated; but it is easy for the politician and the administrator to go to the other extreme and to forget that John Smith has his own affairs. A problem is not the less important because it is a personal problem, nor a service less important because it is a local service.

Inevitably, though, national affairs occupy the centre of the stage. These are in charge of an odd combination of amateur and professional administrators, the amateurs controlling the professionals.

THE CIVIL SERVICE

The average civil servant has probably forgotten why he is so called. He is an officer of one of Her Majesty's Civil Establishments, which are distinguished from Her Majesty's Naval, Military, and Air Force Establishments. He is, in other words, a civil servant because he is a civilian employee, not subject to naval, military, or Air Force discipline. The exact point at which he became a professional can never be ascertained. Technically he is, like his political chief, a servant of the Queen, dismissable at her pleasure. Even if he has what looks like a cast-iron contract – and most civil servants have no contracts at all – he cannot sue for wrongful dismissal unless he is protected by an Act of Parliament. His tenure of office is therefore as insecure as his political chief's. The fact that the politician is as changeable as the climate while the civil servant, like Tennyson's brook, goes on for ever, is simply a product of practice or convention.

The politicians of the eighteenth century did not think of themselves as politicians. They were persons of importance who were interested in affairs of State and who were requested by the monarch to undertake the responsibilities of high office. They were chosen from persons of political importance, peers or Members of Parliament, because the monarch needed a majority in Parliament, and so he chose those who had political influence. They in turn appointed the inferior officers, secretaries, assistant secretaries, clerks, writers, excisemen, dockyard officials, and so on. They could, if they pleased, appoint their relatives, friends, and political supporters. What is more, a new Minister could make a clean sweep by using the Crown's power of dismissal and filling the vacancies with his own men. This 'patronage' was used for political as well as for personal purposes, and the offices which conferred the most patronage, the Treasury, the Admiralty, and the Secretary of State, were politically the most important. The First Lord of the Treasury became Prime Minister because the Treasury had the most patronage and was therefore the most influential politically.

The distribution of patronage among members of Parliament was however limited by an Act of Anne's reign which disqualified from sitting and voting in Parliament a person who was appointed to a new office, created after 1705. Other legislation, designed at first to cut down the royal influence in Parliament, notably an Act of 1741 and Burke's Economy Act of 1782, reduced the number of offices which might be held by Members of Parliament. Consequently, a distinction was drawn between offices which might be held by Members of Parliament and those which might not.

This development did not in itself make a distinction between politicians who were 'transient and embarrassed phantoms' and permanent officials. No officials were permanent so long as patronage prevailed. The disappearance of patronage was due not to legislation but to administrative reforms carried out mainly under Pitt, Peel, and Gladstone. In the early stage the change was purely one of practice. A new political head made no change among the staff of his department. A further change was consequential upon Macaulay's advocacy of selection by competitive examination. On Macaulay's insistence it was applied to the Indian Civil Service, one of the largest and most fruitful branches of patronage, in 1833. The 'examination-wallahs' were much criticized, and the system was not applied to the United Kingdom until 1855, when the Civil Service Commission was established. The Commission was authorized to grant certificates of competence to candidates for junior posts and to hold examinations for persons nominated by the departments. The creation of a system of pensions under the Superannuation Act, 1859, encouraged the generalization of this arrangement; and since 1870 most vacancies in the public service, other than those requiring professional or technical qualifications, and excepting the 'industrial workers', have been filled by examination.

The civil service is now organized into classes, recruited, mainly by examination, at the various education levels. The most important is the administrative class, which is recruited from the universities, and which is primarily responsible, under ministerial control, for the formulation and execution of the Government's policy. It says much for Victorian traditions that a service which grew out of patronage should have established and maintained a reputation for honesty as great as that of Her Majesty's judges. Its intellectual quality, too, is very high. It does not recruit quite the ablest intellectually of each generation, for they become scholars, scientists, and professional men: but it does secure nearly the best. What is more, it prefers and usually secures men and women with first classes or good second classes whose education has been broad and general and not merely specialized. The public schools and the residential universities, whatever their defects, do succeed in producing young men and women with character and maturing judgement who have, at least in the past, made good civil servants.

The popular newspapers make allegations about procrastination, lack of imagination, and 'red tape', but they are not entirely justified. It is true that a decision on an important issue may take time. A business man may be able to gamble on his 'hunch' because he makes profits on the swings when he suffers losses on the roundabouts. A civil servant must not make a mistake because he is acting on behalf of his Minister, and neither a Minister nor a civil servant can balance his successes against his failures. It is usually necessary, therefore, for two or more civil servants to be consulted, and this process takes time. 'Red tape' is commonly associated with financial control. The business man can risk losses provided he makes a sufficient profit over the year. The public and the House of Commons rightly insist that there shall be no losses of public funds. Financial 'red tape' has been laid down not so much by the Treasury as by the Public Accounts Committee of the House of Commons, a body which has been meeting for over a hundred years and has developed a whole volume of rules and precautions which it expects the Treasury and the Comptroller and Auditor General to enforce against the departments.

These restrictions affect the speed and efficiency of administration not through defects in the civil servants but through the very nature of public administration. They are strong reasons for not asking the civil service to do too much. When the State engages in trade or industry it has to use the methods of trade or industry, not the methods of the civil service. The civil servant's concern is with policy, and in this sphere it cannot be alleged that he is lacking in imagination. On the contrary, anybody who consistently follows a line of policy, be it foreign affairs, or colonial policy, or finance, or social welfare, must frequently be amazed at the fertility of imagination shown by the civil service. There are few political problems to which there are obvious solutions, for if the solutions were obvious they would not be problems. Any outside expert who asks himself what steps he would recommend if the responsibility for giving advice to Ministers were vested in him frequently finds a better recommendation coming up from the civil service. Nor is there usually much delay. In foreign affairs particularly a decision has often to be taken on the spur of the moment.

Nor can it be alleged that the civil service is overstaffed and overpaid. It may indeed be more truly alleged that the service is understaffed and underpaid. The senior administrator can seldom relax. The problems keep coming before him and he has to find solutions. If he is driving a car or washing up or playing golf his mind is formulating the minutes which he has to write next day. The difficulty is that so many minutes have to be written. It is impossible to make a sub-division of labour because all the problems of government are connected with each other. Overwork is therefore endemic in the senior ranks of the civil service and is an inevitable part of the system. In return for this overwork the civil servant receives a salary which is perhaps one-third of what he could earn outside the public service. It is not only proper but essential for the efficiency of the service that he should retire as soon as his mind loses its elasticity, be allowed to live in modest comfort on his pension, and be honoured by the Queen with a K.C.B. or a K.C.M.G.

MINISTERIAL CONTROL

The older system of government, so far as it was a system, was government by amateurs. The great lord or the scion of a noble house who was called to the King's service governed the country as he governed, or would govern, his estates. He was, so to speak, born to rule. With that capacity to adapt institutions to meet new objectives which is characteristic of the English, the amateur has remained an amateur. He may be a Cecil or a Percy, or he may be a

Smith or a Jones; he may be a great landowner or a trade unionist; he may have derived his education from Eton and King's or from a council school and experience; he is still an amateur. He differs from his predecessors in that he has to be a politician, an active member of the party in power, and usually (though some of the Ministers are peers of the second or older generation) a person who has thought fit to offer himself as candidate for a parliamentary election and has been thought suitable by a constituency party. His task is to see that the policy followed by his Ministry accords with the policy of Her Majesty's Government and therefore with the policy of the party which won the last election.

As we shall see later, when a political leader is commissioned by the Queen to form a Government, he has something like a hundred offices to fill. At the Treasury he has to provide a Chancellor of the Exchequer, a Financial Secretary, and several Lords. At the Foreign Office he needs a Secretary of State and a Parliamentary Under-Secretary of State. At the Board of Trade he needs a President and a Parliamentary Secretary. At the Ministry of Education he requires a Minister and a Parliamentary Secretary. The list is not precisely fixed. He may decide that Health and Local Government should be associated, or that Housing and Town and Country Planning should be separated, or that Industry should be separated from Trade and associated with Labour. Somehow, though, he has to provide for political control of all the fields of central administration. The civil servants run the machine, but somebody must control each of the branches in order to ensure responsibility to the House of Commons and thence to the electorate.

This responsibility is assumed in two ways. In the first place, all questions of political importance are submitted to the Minister for his personal decision. One of the duties of a good civil servant is to know both what to submit and what not to submit. The volume of work in every large Ministry is immense. It varies, however, in political importance. At the one extreme is the Foreign Office, where there is a very high proportion of questions which may give rise to political disputes; at the other extreme is the Post Office, where most decisions are of an executive character and require no great exercise of discretion. If the Minister tries to deal with even a tithe of the daily questions he will find himself swamped in paper work and committee discussions. What he has to do, and what his professional advisers have to help him to do, is to select those questions which are of sufficient importance to justify his personal attention. He receives assistance from his Parliamentary Secretary, who may be given and usually is given a special field or group of fields in which he acts on behalf of the Minister.

It must be remembered that Ministers are not professional administrators. Some, like the late Viscount Snowden, became good administrators. Others – of whom John Bright was the outstanding example – never learn. Administration cannot be taught, but every administrator knows that it can be learned. What is wanted primarily is an odd quality called 'judgement'. It is not easy to describe, for it is more easily appreciated than analysed. It consists partly in being able to go to the root of a problem, to find out where its essence lies. Most problems of government are complex, for when a stone is thrown into a pond waves are sent out in all directions. The inexpert administrator tries to foresee and to meet all the possible complications, and very often he produces a complex and 'clever' solution. The expert puts his finger on the centre of disturbance and presses in the direction which will ease the situation. Some politicians are very good at this kind of thing, for in the course of political controversy every problem becomes oversimplified. On a broad economic problem, like free trade, on which an economist would like to write a book, the politician has to make a speech which will be understood in Mile End or Bournemouth. The speech will be a contribution to the problem only if it sticks to essentials.

Usually the simplest solution is the best solution: but even if it is not, it is usually the only acceptable solution, because its import has to be understood by ordinary people. The good administrator knows, by experience if not by instinct, how the mind of the ordinary man will react. Sir Winston

Churchill could hardly be described as an expert on strategy, but it was unnecessary for him to decide in 1940 whether Britain had the means to fight on. His impulse was to fight with whatever means were available, and he followed his impulse. Hitler similarly relied on his intuition, but he lacked the quality which we are trying to analyse. He was clever, but his judgement was faulty.

Nor must it be forgotten that the Minister is only a part-time administrator. He is also a Member of Parliament, and he must spend much of his time making and listening to speeches at Westminster. He must keep touch with his constituency. He must be able to take part in the general party propaganda and to attend party conferences. He must be accessible to all those who are politically important. He must take part in all kinds of formal and informal functions. A Foreign Secretary cannot refuse to see the Ambassador from Ruritania merely because he thinks His Excellency an old bore and Ruritanian problems of no importance. He must attend the party to celebrate the Ruritanian National Day and, perhaps, say something pleasant which will not annoy Urbania.

It follows that the Minister must not be given too many questions to decide. Somebody must decide what questions are important enough and what are not. In large measure, the answer is to be found in political conditions. The Minister and his advisers have to watch two sections of opinion, that of his party and that of the Opposition. The party consists not of the millions of people who voted for the Prime Minister at the last election, but of the few thousands who take an active part in politics. They have ideas of their own, crude ideas very often, but ideas which they expect their Goverment to put into practice. Politically speaking, they are the salt of the earth, for they enable the party to win elections. If they feel strongly on any issue, that issue is inevitably of political importance, and the Minister concerned must make certain that the issue is decided the right way. He may have to say to his advisers: 'How right you are; but I have to carry the party.'

The Opposition is even more important, because it may

be able to make a molehill look like a mountain. If a question is of sufficient public interest it will be raised in the House of Commons; and if it is raised in the House the Minister must deal with it. It may be enough for him to read a prepared brief, but he must at least understand the brief, for he may have to deal with supplementary questions or interjections. There is an official in the 'box' just outside the confines of the House to help him, but the Minister is far away on the Front Bench and he must not too obviously be in the hands of his officials. It is true that many questions raised in the House are not of general importance. Members have to satisfy their constituents, and purely local or personal issues are often raised in their behalf at question time. Even so, what appears to be a local or personal question may raise large issues. Particularly is this so if questions of personal liberty arise, for the House has always shown itself critical of invasions of personal liberty, even in what appear at first sight to be unpromising cases.

In taking decisions the Minister must remember that he is acting in the name of and on behalf of the Government. His action pledges his colleagues, their supporters in the House of Commons, and the party as a whole. If a question is sufficiently important, he must refer it to the Cabinet. Even if it is not he must so decide that the political stability of the Government and the popular support of his party are not affected.

Even the hardest-working Minister cannot take a tithe of the decisions which present themselves for decision. Those which cannot be put to him must be decided by officials, at the level of the Under-Secretaries or the Assistant Secretaries. Their decisions are, however, the decisions of the Minister and he cannot subsequently repudiate them. They must be decisions of such a character that they would have been taken by him if he had had time to deal with them. They carry the same implications as his own. They are the decisions of Her Majesty's Government, capable of causing as much political difficulty as those of the Minister or the Cabinet. The Minister and his colleagues must be able to defend them in the House of Commons, to justify them to their party organizations, and to persuade the electors that they are not harmful. The officials must therefore study Government policy and appreciate the criticisms that might be made by the Opposition.

It is true that there is what may be called a 'departmental policy', a policy carrying no particular political implications, but developed by experience of administration. It varies little from Government to Government. It can of course be changed if opposition develops to it, but party policy is usually an adaptation of departmental policy. The emphasis may change with the Government, but the substance remains the same. This is particularly true in external affairs and defence. The social, economic, and political conditions which produce policy do not vary from Government to Government. The one party may be more favourable to the Soviet Union, or more anxious to provide armaments, or more eager to use tariffs, than the other: but essentially the objectives are the same. Even so, the official must remember that he is acting for Her Majesty's Government, and that his decision may become a source of political controversy.

THE MINISTRY AND THE CABINET

IN the previous chapter the process of government was examined from the bottom to the top; fully to understand the process it must be studied also from the top to the bottom. The latter is the more familiar process; because the Ministers get the publicity it is assumed that they play a larger part than they actually do. Most proposals which result in Cabinet decisions come from the Departments. The civil service governs; the Ministers control the process of government.

When the Queen sends for a party leader and he agrees to form a Government as Prime Minister, he has to advise the making of about one hundred appointments which are recognized to be political and which are filled by members of his party in both Houses of Parliament. They vary from the great offices of State, the key positions in the Government such as the Foreign Office, the Treasury, the Home Office, the Woolsack (the office of the Lord Chancellor), and the Ministry of Defence, to minor posts like the lordships of the Treasury (held by the Government Whips) and certain appointments in the Royal Household. As usual in the British Constitution, there is no logic in the division between political appointments and permanent appointments. The holders of political appointments take part in the political work of the Government, but it does not always follow that the holder of a political office has to take or assist in the taking of political decisions of importance. The Lord Chancellor is, in the main, a judge and the president of the House of Lords; the Lord President of the Council holds an office of great honour whose functions are mainly formal and technical; the Lord Privy Seal has no function at all unless some special job is assigned to him; the Chancellor of the Duchy of Lancaster is said to have about one and a half hours of work a week, and it can hardly be regarded as important. These offices, except that of Lord

Chancellor which requires high legal ability and wide experience, are generally held by men who are wise in counsel or, what comes to the same thing, important in politics. One of them may be Leader of the House of Commons or Deputy Prime Minister; all of them will probably be useful on Cabinet committees, whose work is heavy.

Our attention must however be directed mainly towards the Ministers who have heavy Departmental duties. It is impossible to be precise about the number, because it varies from Government to Government according as the Prime Minister thinks that the work ought to be distributed. There are, too, other aspects of his problem. He has to find jobs for his more prominent political supporters because one of his functions is to keep his party together, and he must satisfy all sections of party opinion even if his opinions about the sectional leaders are unprintable. Also, if public opinion is agitated about a particular problem like housing – or, what comes to the same thing, if the Opposition considers that this problem offers a fruitful line of criticism – it may be desirable for the Prime Minister to allocate a Minister to take charge of that problem. The Minister is expected to solve it, or at least to give the appearance of great activity in attempting to solve it. There are, however, about twenty-four or twenty-five Departments with substantial duties.

In the days when Departments were not so numerous, all the Ministers at the head of important Departments were members of the Cabinet. In addition, there were several Ministers, holding the more or less honorary offices already mentioned, who were summoned to the Cabinet because their advice was weighty or their political influence considerable. As the State assumed more and more responsibilities, the number of Ministers grew; and as the numbers of Ministers grew the Cabinet became larger. Sir Robert Peel in 1841 had a Cabinet of fourteen, of whom five had light Departmental duties or none at all; Disraeli in 1874 had a Cabinet of twelve, of whom one had light duties and one had none at all; Sir Henry Campbell-Bannerman in 1906 had a Cabinet of nineteen, of whom three had no heavy Departmental duties; Baldwin in 1935 had a Cabinet of twenty-two, of whom four had no heavy Departmental duties.

The Cabinet has to take decisions in all matters of major importance which cannot be disposed of at a lower level. Roughly it may be said that a question has to go to the Cabinet if it is the subject of acute political controversy or it raises inter-departmental questions and the Departments concerned cannot agree. It is therefore necessary to have in the Cabinet all the prominent politicians of the party; but it is also convenient to have there all the Heads of Departments whose functions have or may have political importance. Since the actions of a Minister implicate the whole Government, it is important that he should know the general trend of Government policy. A Minister of Fuel and Power, for instance, ought to know a good deal about economic policy. On the other hand, a large Cabinet is a different sort of machine from a small Cabinet. A Cabinet of twelve persons, like Disraeli's in 1874, can settle questions by intimate discussion around a table. A Cabinet of twenty-three, like Wilson's in 1964, is verging upon a public meeting: it must have a formal procedure, a considerable committee orgánization, a substantial secretariat, and so on. A small Cabinet can usually take decisions by a consensus of opinion; a large Cabinet may find it easier to take a vote.

Experienced politicians prefer the small Cabinet, but they have not been very good at explaining why. The committee work of a large Cabinet must occupy a good deal of time, but that time is determined primarily by the complexities of government. The length of a discussion in the Cabinet or a Cabinet Committee must depend primarily on the people present, whether they have ideas of their own, or ambitions of their own. The influence of the Prime Minister may be greater in a large Cabinet or a small one, as the case may be. In short it seems impossible to generalize about the advantages and disadvantages of a small Cabinet. Too much depends upon the personalities of its members.

The size of the Cabinet cannot be reduced unless some Departmental Ministers are left out. It became usual to leave out the Postmaster-General and the First Commissioner of Works (now superseded by the Minister of Works). The Ministry of Transport, when first created in 1919, was thought not to be important enough to be represented in the Cabinet. The Minister of Pensions has almost invariably been outside the Cabinet. In the post-war Cabinets the Ministers of Food, Town and Country Planning, National Insurance, Supply, Power, Public Works and Civil Aviation have generally been left out.

The creation of the Ministry of Defence in 1940 made a further reduction possible and established a principle which could be widened. The Minister of Defence did not take over the functions of the First Lord of the Admiralty, the Secretary of State for War, and the Secretary of State for Air. He was responsible for common defence policy and what may be called the strategic balance among the sea, land, and air forces. In consequence it is possible for the Minister of Defence to represent all three services in the Cabinet and for the Ministers in charge of the Admiralty, the War Office, and the Air Ministry to remain outside. This was the first application of a principle which had been much discussed before the war, that of having a co-ordinating Minister over a group of Departments, settling common and inter-departmental policy and representing the Departments in the Cabinet. Generally, opinion was against this scheme because it threatened to add to the growing complexity of government. A superior Minister implies a superior Ministry. A proposal having been fully discussed by one set of officials and settled by one Minister, is then discussed by another set of officials and settled by another Minister. It is always easy to add to the work without adding to the work done. Nevertheless, the precedent having been set by Churchill during the war, he followed it in his Government of 1951. A Secretary of State for the Co-ordination of Transport, Fuel and Power was appointed, and the Lord President of the Council was charged with the co-ordination of the Ministries of Food and Agriculture. The office of Paymaster-General, which in itself is a sinecure, was used to provide a Minister to co-ordinate scientific research and development. Since all these were peers, they were described by Mr Churchill's critics as 'the overlords'.

For a time these devices kept down the size of Cabinets. Attlee in 1950 had eighteen members, while Churchill in 1951 had sixteen: but Home had twenty-two and Wilson in 1964 had twenty-three. Outside Wilson's Cabinet of 1964 were twenty-one Ministers, of whom seven were Ministers of State, Ministers appointed to assist heavily-burdened Ministers by taking over some of their functions. Since Ministers not in the Cabinet attend when matters affecting their Departments are discussed, the size of the Cabinet has substantially increased.

Churchill's 'overlords' were not a success, partly because they were lords and not commoners. The Ministry of Defence now has three subordinate Ministers of Defence for the Army, the Royal Air Force and the Royal Navy, but the responsibility is vested in the Minister. There was something like 'overlordship' in Wilson's Cabinet of 1964: but speaking generally nobody likes 'overlords'. It may be doubted if they like themselves.

COLLECTIVE RESPONSIBILITY

Cabinet government is government by committee, but it differs from ordinary committee government because, through the party system, an attempt is made to achieve uniformity of political opinion. Usually a committee, whether it be a Select Committee of the House of Commons, a local education committee, or the committee of a sports club, contains members whose opinions differ widely. After discussion a vote is taken on a motion, and if the motion is approved by the majority it becomes the decision of the committee. Even if a member finds himself consistently in a minority he does not resign: he carries on arguing for lost causes.

The Cabinet is not such a committee. Normally, it is chosen from among the members of one party, who accept the party policy as a matter of course. Though it may take a decision by a majority vote, a member who found himself consistently in a minority would wish to resign, and indeed he would be asked to do so. There are, of course, shades of opinion in a party, stretching from the left wing to the right wing, the progressive wing to the conservative wing, the active wing to the passive wing: but there is fundamental agreement over principles, and the disagreement is over emphasis. Usually a Prime Minister does his best to get both wings into the Cabinet and to reach decisions by compromise. A Cabinet split may become a party split and a party split may lose the next election. The parties are so nicely balanced that if the one loses support and the other gains it the Opposition may obtain the majority.

Whatever the decision, a Minister who remains in the Cabinet must accept it. It becomes his decision as much as that of his colleagues. This idea of collective responsibility developed in the eighteenth century as a protection for Ministers against the King. Though technically the Cabinet is and always has been the creature of the Prime Minister, the Ministers as such were appointed and dismissed by the King. If the Ministers regarded themselves as individual advisers of the King, he could play off one against another and, subject always to the need for a majority in the House of Commons, keep Government policy under his control. If the Ministers stuck together and insisted on giving collective advice, the King had either to accept that advice or find an alternative Government, and if the Cabinet still stuck together, the alternative Government had to be found among the Opposition. Since party lines were not then very strict and both parties were divided into groups, the King might be able to get his way: but obviously the task was more difficult than it would have been if he had been able to break up the Government. Hence the Cabinet presented what is now called a common front.

A Minister was, however, answerable to the House of Commons as well as to the King. The House voted expenditure and insisted on its right to criticize the policy implicit in that expenditure. This expenditure was apportioned among the Ministries, and the House could express its disapproval of the policy of a Ministry by voting against an appropriate item of the Estimates. If the Minister regarded himself as personally responsible, he would have to resign. If the Government as a whole regarded itself as responsible the Government would resign. To turn out the Government was a more serious matter than to turn out a Minister. In the course of the nineteenth century, too, the private member relied more and more on his party support and less and less on his 'influence' or the 'influence' of his patron in his constituency. He would lose the party support if he helped to turn out the Government. Hence collective responsibility became a device for maintaining the strength and the unity of the party.

Collective responsibility applies particularly to the Cabinet. It means, in principle, that the individual members of the Cabinet accept complete responsibility for the decisions of the Cabinet. It is associated with the cognate principle of Cabinet secrecy, which has both a different origin and a different justification. Cabinet secrecy takes its origin from the fact that the Ministers are appointed to advise the King. That advice is, or was, secret for the same reason that the advice of a legal or medical adviser is secret. One does not expect one's lawyer or doctor or banker or stockbroker to noise abroad what advice he has given. If counsel advises that a case is not very strong but is worth fighting, the client does not expect that he will give that opinion to the other side. The Minister is in fact sworn of the Privy Council in order that he may be bound by the oath of secrecy which all Privy Counsellors are required to take. The reason for secrecy has changed, however, just as the reason for collective responsibility has changed. The Cabinet is a secret meeting of Ministers at which they decide what policy shall be followed. It is essential that they should speak freely and frankly, toss their thoughts across the table, make tentative propositions and withdraw them when the difficulties are pointed out, express their doubts without reserve, discuss personalities as well as principles. This kind of discussion, the only sort of discussion which produces satisfactory conclusions, cannot be conducted in public. Nor can anybody express his opinions without reserve if he may find them being quoted in Parliament or published in the press. The senate of a university, the selection committee of a football club, the stewards of a race meeting, the directors of a company find it equally necessary to maintain secrecy. In politics such secrecy is even more important, for a politician lives on publicity and a party depends on public opinion. It is therefore essential that the Cabinet should decide not only what it proposes to do but also what it proposes to say. Its decision has to be one which its members can defend in public, but they must not allow their tentative opinions and casual remarks to be used for propaganda purposes by their opponents; they cannot reach the best decisions because they dare not speak their minds if there is a chance that what they speak will be broadcast.

Collective responsibility means, then, that an attack on a Minister is an attack on the Government. The defeat of a Minister is the defeat of the Government. It also means that the members of the Cabinet express a common opinion. To use the phrase said to have been used by Lord Melbourne, Queen Victoria's first Prime Minister, 'they must all be in the same story'.

It follows, too, that a Minister may not disclose what he said or proposed, or what anybody else said or proposed, in the Cabinet. There is one exception to this rule. When a Minister finds himself unable to agree with a Cabinet decision and resigns, it is obviously just that he should be allowed to say why he resigned, and in order to do so he must be able to disclose Cabinet discussions. He therefore asks the Queen's permission, through the Prime Minister, to state his case. The permission is usually given, but it is limited to the explanation of the circumstances which led to his resignation. He must not disclose other occasions on which he differed from the rest of the Cabinet. This is an important precaution. Usually the issue on which a Cabinet Minister resigns is not an isolated incident. It is the culmination of a series of disagreements, the straw which broke the camel's back. If he gives a long history of disagreement the other members must disclose why they disagreed with him, and much of the procedure of the Cabinet will inevitably come into public discussion. Such discussion is not merely unfortunate for the party in power; it is undesirable in the public interest; for if there is a risk that his remarks will be disclosed, no Minister will be able to speak freely and frankly.

Collective responsibility covers more than the decisions of the Cabinet. Matters are not taken to the Cabinet unless they are of sufficient political importance or they involve conflicts of opinion between Departments which cannot be settled at lower levels. Questions which do not come within these categories are decided by Ministers or by civil servants on their behalf. We have already seen that decisions are taken by civil servants on behalf of their Ministers, and that the decisions of Ministers are taken on behalf of the Cabinet. The policy of the Government thus permeates the whole administration and the Cabinet accepts collective responsibility for it. The principle must not be carried too far. If a Metropolitan policeman – who, unlike policemen outside the Metropolis, is a servant of the Crown – takes a bribe, the House of Commons does not allege that the Cabinet has taken a bribe. What it may say is that the Cabinet is at fault in allowing corruption to enter the Metropolitan Police. Also, there have been cases in which Ministers have accepted personal responsibility for errors of judgement by themselves or their subordinates and have tendered their resignations. In 1917 the Royal Commission on Mesopotamia passed adverse comments on the administration of the India Office, whereupon the Secretary of State, Austen Chamberlain, resigned. In 1935 Sir Samuel Hoare accepted personal responsibility for his agreement with M. Laval over Abyssinia, and resigned. In this case there was express Cabinet approval, but Sir Samuel offered himself as a scapegoat in order to divert public disapproval from the Government.

It follows from the principle of collective responsibility that parliamentary criticism ought to be directed not against a civil servant or a Minister but against the Government as a whole. So far as the civil service is concerned the principle is applied. The civil servant acting as such is not criticized, and indeed the civil service does its best to remain anonymous. It is impossible to keep that anonymity in foreign affairs. It is safe to say that not one man in a hundred thousand knows the name of the Permanent Under-Secretary of State for Foreign Affairs – the official head of the Foreign Office – but it is sometimes necessary for officials to make speeches on United Nations Commissions. In the colonies, too, the names of the local officials are necessarily known and the efficiency of their work is canvassed in the local press. In consequence it is occasionally necessary ostentatiously to recall a Governor, thus throwing on him the responsibility for defects of administration. The doctrine of collective responsibility is not pushed so far as to become a fiction. If a riot breaks out in Swaziland the Government may be blamed for the conditions which caused it, but it can hardly avoid disclosing that the situation would not have got out of hand if the District Commissioner had been efficient.

The Minister in charge is by no means anonymous. He probably glories in the publicity he receives and he is rarely modest about his achievements or even about the achievements of his subordinates. If the theory of collective responsibility were fully carried out, he would ascribe his success to the Government. This would be too much to expect. What is more, while the Opposition blames the Government through the Minister, it does not hesitate to blame the Minister. In every Government there are Ministers who are especially susceptible to attack, either because the problems of their Departments are difficult or because they are inexpert in dealing with parliamentary criticisms. Political propaganda is to be made by attacking them, and they do get attacked. They are, however, defended by other Ministers, and the attack is really aimed not at the Ministers but at the Government. It may be convenient for the Prime Minister to promote a difficult Minister to a different office; but that is not the Opposition's intention: their principal anxiety is to cause the Government to lose votes at the next election.

This brings us to the essence of collective responsibility

What it means in theory is that if the House of Commons disapproves of the action of the Government, or of any part of it, the House can express its lack of confidence in the Government and compel it either to resign or to dissolve Parliament. Given the party system, however, this is something of a fiction. In all normal circumstances the majority will support the Government because it is a party majority and the Government is a party Government. The Opposition has no real hope of defeating it in Parliament; what it hopes to do is to defeat it in the constituencies at the next opportunity. The criticism aims at a gradual change of opinion.

The technique is embodied in the Greek proverb that constant dripping wears away the stone. Even the most loyal supporter must sometimes disagree with his party, and the average elector is not a loyal supporter but just a person who normally votes Conservative or Labour. If his disagreement on a political question can be made a little more emphatic by effective criticism; if his disagreement on a few questions can be converted by sustained propaganda into disagreement on many issues; then the Opposition may have got so far as to dissuade him from voting for the Government even if it has not persuaded him to vote against it. What is more, discontent grows like a snowball. It passes around the pub and the club, the canteen and the office, the train and the tram, and ends up in the ballot box.

If the Government's defence is to be effective collective responsibility is essential. Whatever the differences may be in private they must not be made public. Nor can the Minister particularly attacked be left to defend himself: he must be given support both in Parliament and outside. Normally this support would be given by his colleagues in the Cabinet, but the Prime Minister has by convention the right to call on members of his Ministry to support the Government both by voice and by vote. A Parliamentary Secretary or Junior Minister who disagreed with an item of Government policy would perhaps be allowed quietly to abstain from voting, but he is normally expected to assume that, if he had been in the Cabinet and had heard the discussion, he would have acquiesced.

Collective responsibility is not an easy system to operate, especially in the rawer democracies outside the United Kingdom. It assumes the team spirit of Rugby football, or of a well-drilled dramatic cast. Politicians are apt to think of themselves, in the language of the cinema, as 'stars' and to seek publicity for themselves instead of for the Government. It is not easy for, say, the Minister of Education to appreciate that he has no policy other than the policy of Her Majesty's Government, that he must speak for the Government and not for himself and, if his Department is successful, that he must give the credit to the Government instead of taking it for himself.

CABINET PROCEDURE

Before the war, the Cabinet used to meet for two hours a week for about forty weeks in the year. Since the war, there have usually been two meetings a week. Considering the vast complexities of Government, it may seem surprising that the meetings are so few and so short. The problem of increasing business has been met by delegation and by better organization of business.

The principle of collective responsibility enables the Departments to limit the number of problems put to the Cabinet. The Assistant Secretary acts on behalf of and in the name of his Minister; the Minister acts on behalf of and in the name of Her Majesty's Government. Hence the function of the Assistant Secretary is to take the decision which the Cabinet would have taken if he had put up a memorandum and asked for a Cabinet ruling. If he is in doubt he can ask for the Minister's ruling. Only where the matter is of the highest political importance or where two Departments differ is it necessary to seek a Cabinet decision.

The Departments often do differ. The business of Government does not fall neatly into twenty-five or more compartments. Foreign policy affects trade and trade affects foreign policy; food and agriculture are cognate subjects (so much so that they now have an 'overlord'); transport, fuel, trade, supply, and economic policy are often merely different aspects of the same problem; the social services hang together; above all, nearly every problem is a financial problem, and every Department is in constant consultation with the Treasury; every problem is also a problem of staff, and therefore a problem in which the Establishments Branch of the Treasury is involved.

It must not be thought that the relations among the Departments involve a state of perpetual warfare. On the contrary, the normal process is one of consultation and common action. The official concerned talks to his 'opposite number' on the telephone, or goes round to see him, or asks his concurrence in a memorandum. Every conflict involves more work for the official; and, since every senior official tends to be overworked, it is in his own interest to keep differences few. If a difference of opinion does develop, an informal conference or a more formal inter-departmental committee may be able to solve it. If need be the Ministers are brought into the discussion. Only in the last resort is the problem taken to the Cabinet; and if the question is of minor importance the Cabinet's response may be that the Departments should settle it among themselves.

Even if the matter is put to the Cabinet, it will probably be referred to a Cabinet committee. Though there were occasionally Cabinet committees during the nineteenth century, their development as a regular part of the machine came in the present century. In the main the development was associated with the Committee of Imperial Defence, now known as the Defence Committee, which settled defence problems, subject to Cabinet control, before the war of 1914 and between the wars. It was not a Cabinet committee but a committee appointed by the Prime Minister. It functioned, however, through a network of committees and sub-committees and had, unlike the Cabinet, a permanent secretariat. In 1916 it was absorbed by the War Cabinet, committees and sub-committees and secretariat and all, with the result that the committee system, which was tending to develop independently through pressure of business, became a regular part of the process of government in Cabinet. There are standing committees for matters which arise frequently and *ad hoc* committees for special problems. On one occasion when a check was made, before the war of 1939-45, it was found that the Chancellor of the Exchequer was a member of eleven Cabinet committees. It is unlikely that committee business has declined since the war. Exceptions apart, the names and functions of Cabinet committees are not disclosed because they would indicate some of the more important business under Cabinet discussion. For instance, one of the committees of the pre-1914 Committee of Imperial Defence dealt with naval operations in the neighbourhood of a foreign country. If the functions of the committee had been disclosed not only that foreign country but several naval powers would have set their Intelligence organizations at work to discover why the Royal Navy was working out plans in that particular region.

The presence in the Cabinet of several Ministers without heavy Departmental duties is justified not only by the assistance which they can give in Cabinet discussions but also by the fact that they can act as chairmen of Cabinet committees and so relieve the Departmental Ministers of some of the heavy committee work. Also, Ministers who are not of the Cabinet, Parliamentary Secretaries, and even officials can sit on Cabinet committees. Even so, the more important committees must contain the more important Ministers, and it is this heavy committee work, added to heavy Departmental work and parliamentary duties, which causes so much pressure on Ministers.

The pressure can be relieved by a well-organized secretariat. Oddly enough, there was no secretariat at all until 1916. So secret were Cabinet decisions that Ministers were not allowed to take notes. The Prime Minister kept an informal agenda before him and made rough notes upon which he based his letter to the monarch explaining the Cabinet decisions. Apart from that letter there was no record of Cabinet decisions. Ministers went back to their

Departments to give the necessary instructions on the basis
of their recollections. Sometimes, especially when there was
acute controversy, Ministers had to ask each other afterwards what really had been decided. Though the Committee of Imperial Defence was an equally secret body, its
highly complex organization made a secretariat essential.
When that organization was absorbed in the War Cabinet
in 1916 the secretariat was taken over. Indeed the War
Cabinet could not have functioned without it. When the
Coalition Government disappeared in 1922 there was a
proposal to abolish the secretariat, but wiser counsels prevailed, and the modern Cabinet, with its network of
committees, could not function without it.

The secretariat assists the despatch of business in several
ways. In the first place, it compiles an agenda which enables
the Prime Minister to ensure that every question ripe for
decision is brought up. In the second place, it secures from
the Departments the memoranda necessary to explain the
items of the agenda. By the time a question reaches the
Cabinet it has been very fully discussed and the points at
issue can be set out very shortly. The Cabinet is concerned
with principles and not with details. Those details ought to
have been worked out because, as every administrator
knows, a bright idea which has never been thought out
often proves to be impracticable. On the other hand, they
are not the concern of the Cabinet, and so only a short
memorandum setting out a proposal, or alternative proposals, is needed. In the third place, the secretariat makes
certain that those Ministers who are not of the Cabinet
attend at the right time for the discussion of items in which
they are concerned. In the fourth place, by asking what
conclusions have to be recorded, the secretariat makes
certain that all the questions under discussion are fully
disposed of. Finally, the conclusions or 'minutes' can be
circulated to the Departments so that action can be taken
by them in accordance with Cabinet decisions.

A similar procedure applies to Cabinet committees, which
sometimes have power to dispose of questions and sometimes merely report to the Cabinet.

GOVERNMENT AND OPINION

It is essential to remember the context in which the Cabinet reaches its conclusions. The problems placed before it almost invariably come from the Departments. They may have been part of the party programme or may have arisen through the operation of events which compel Ministers to initiate discussions. More often they arise out of administration, the initiative being taken by the officials concerned with the administration. In any case the decisions taken are subject to the very real threat of parliamentary criticism. How the Opposition functions has already been explained. Its purpose being to make the Government unpopular in order that it may lose votes at the next election, it scrutinizes every Government decision to find out what elements in it are open to criticism. It has quasi-experts who follow closely the various fields of Government policy. Probably it is able to call on outside experts who are in sympathy with the Opposition and who are able to base criticism on technical knowledge and experience. It is at least as closely in touch with the constituencies as the Government and can find out where the shoe pinches. It can inspire leading articles in the daily press and criticism in the weekly reviews. Mainly, though, its criticism is concentrated in the House of Commons itself. It compels the Government to explain and defend itself. It gives a lead to the press on both sides of the political fence. On the one hand it gives expression to public opinion; on the other hand it helps to create public opinion.

Every Government has to take decisions which it knows to be unpopular, because it believes that other decisions would prove to be even more unpopular. Nobody likes 'austerity', but there is even greater dislike of unemployment, lower wages, longer hours of work, and other consequences of trade depression. The simple solution of inflating currency is not likely to be immediately unpopular, but the volume of criticism will become large as soon as prices begin to rise. A Government which takes the easy way will meet prophecies of woe on the Opposition benches, and if those prophecies are fulfilled public opinion may swing towards the Opposition. One effect of Opposition, therefore, is to keep the Government along the strait and narrow path of honest administration. Such Opposition is not always successful, for the Government like Micawber may hope that something will turn up: and sometimes it does. Another effect of Opposition is that the Government has to explain and defend itself. Every one of its actions may become the subject of political argument.

This argument across the floor of the House of Commons, though theoretically designed to capture votes in the House itself, is in reality addressed to the electorate. The Government seeks to maintain its majority and the Opposition to destroy it. There is of course danger in this appeal to public opinion. Since everybody prefers butter to guns the Government may be tempted to provide butter when it ought to provide guns, and the Opposition may be tempted to argue that, if it were in power, there would be more and better butter, though an honest man on either side of the House would say, if he could consider the matter without thinking of temporary party advantage, that what was needed was more guns. Nobody is so blind as the man who will not see, and we all tend to hope for the best. It is easier to assume that we can eat, drink and be merry this week because something will turn up next week. Thousands back horses and millions enter football pools, though we know that the average man must lose. Political parties are well aware of these tendencies and cannot always risk the temptation to capitalize them for party advantage. Though their economists tell them that they should save in a boom and spend in a depression, what they tend to do is to spend in a boom on the assumption that there will be no depression, and to spend more in a depression (by creating credit) because the boom is just round the corner.

On the other hand, the average man is also a reasonable person and he can be persuaded if the problem is explained to him. A bad democracy is not good merely because it is a democracy; and any form of government that is not a democracy either is bad now or will be bad very soon, for uncontrolled power invariably corrupts those who possess it. On the whole Britain can trust its politicians. They are not always right, but few Governments are prepared to sacrifice the national interest as they see it in order to obtain a present party advantage. Leadership is almost invariably given, and the electorate responds to leadership which it believes to be wise. Government under Opposition criticism has to maintain a close relation with public opinion, but it leads opinion as much as it follows it.

The close division between the parties in the country, which is the special characteristic of British democracy, makes the relationship extremely close. A slight shift of opinion is enough to defeat the Government at the next election. It must therefore be very sensitive to opinion, which expresses itself on the one hand through the party and on the other hand through Parliament.

THE OFFICE

THE office of Prime Minister, like most superior offices, depends very much on what the holder makes of it, though it also depends on tradition and convention. The name itself is French, *premier ministre*, and, like many names in English politics, it was at first a term of abuse. Sir Robert Walpole, who held the office of First Lord of the Treasury from 1721 to 1742, denied the title; and in 1741 the Lords protested against the development of the office. It was, however, a necessary development. George I rarely attended Cabinet meetings not only because of his ignorance of English but also because of his ignorance of English affairs. One of the Ministers necessarily took his place. The effect of his absence must not, however, be exaggerated. Cabinet government had not yet been established and Walpole rarely summoned a full Cabinet because he preferred to work with a few influential Ministers. Walpole's authority depended less on his office than on his personality. George I decided to rely on the Whigs because they could be regarded as wedded to and in fact dependent upon the Hanoverian succession. Walpole was not, in the modern sense, leader of the Whigs, but he was the most influential of them. Even so, his position depended on the King's favour. He needed a majority in Parliament, as his defeat in 1742 and subsequent resignation showed, but in some measure he owed that majority to the King's support. He advised the King on the expenditure of his Civil List and controlled most of the royal patronage. Nor must it be forgotten that, since the King governed, it was unpatriotic to oppose the King's Government. Many might complain that the King chose bad advisers, or that his advisers gave bad advice, but many others would support the Government because they thought it proper to support the King.

Even so, the authority of Parliament increased during

Walpole's long hegemony. George III held back the development for twenty years, but when Lord North was defeated in 1782 through the loss of the American colonies Parliament began to take control. It is significant that the attack was directed mainly against corruption and patronage. William Pitt won the election in 1783 because of the King's support, but thereafter the Prime Minister depended more on Parliament than on the King. He could still rely on 'the King's friends' who would support the King's Minister whoever he might be, but more and more he became a party leader whose strength lay in the support of his party. After 1832 'influence' declined in elections because of the extension of the franchise and the disfranchisement of the smaller boroughs. Electors began to vote for parties and not for the nominees of patrons. Sir Robert Peel's manifesto to the electors of Tamworth in 1834 was in effect an appeal to the people to elect his 'friends'. The party label became one of the most valuable electioneering devices. Organizations were established to secure the registration of party voters and were converted into propaganda machines.

All these developments enhanced the prestige of the party leader, who was for all practical purposes a potential Prime Minister. The conflict between Gladstone and Disraeli, which began with the death of Palmerston in 1865 and ended with Disraeli's death in 1881, added to the power of the office. The party conflict was in large measure a personal conflict. The issue was not only whether the Conservatives or the Liberals should govern Britain but also whether Disraeli or Gladstone should be Prime Minister. The effect of the personal appeal varies according to the personality of the leader. The Labour Party has tended to personify the Party with a capital P and to place less emphasis on the leader. The Conservatives rely heavily on the leader, though less on Home than on Macmillan. Also, the leader may become a liability, like Lloyd George in 1922.

We have seen that the Queen's most important function is to choose a Prime Minister. Usually, she has no real choice. If a party wins the election its leader must become

Prime Minister. Nor has she necessarily much of a choice when a Prime Minister dies or retires while his party retains a majority. Even if formally there is no second-in-command, one of the Ministers usually obtains pre-eminence, is 'groomed' for the post over several years, and steps almost as of right into the post, like Neville Chamberlain in 1937. Even when there is a real choice, as in 1923 (resignation of Bonar Law) or in 1940 (resignation of Neville Chamberlain) it is narrowly limited by political exigencies. The Prime Minister is not merely the Queen's first Minister, nor only the head of the Goverment, but also a party leader, and the Queen must give the party a leader which it is prepared to follow. This will be apparent from a consideration of the Prime Minister's functions.

FUNCTIONS

The Prime Minister is, in the first place, the Queen's private adviser. Though the Queen no longer takes part in politics, she must still be consulted and she may still advise and warn. Her relations with the Prime Minister are therefore close. She keeps in touch with public affairs and requires explanation when matters seem to her to be going wrong. There are times when the prestige of her position may enable her to help. When it was thought wise to make an *entente* with France, Edward VII went to Paris so that his personal popularity might be used to develop a favourable public opinion. In 1921 George V was advised to initiate the movement which led to the settlement of the Irish problem. In 1940 and 1941 George VI made visits to bombed areas in order to maintain morale. The visits which the monarch makes to other parts of the Common-wealth (and the Queen herself was in East Africa when her father died) help to maintain close relations. These are outstanding examples, but it is essential to remember that the Queen is always part of the Government and that her actions are of the greatest importance in maintaining the unity which is characteristic of the British peoples. Disraeli had the imagination to realize the harm caused by Queen

Victoria's withdrawal from public functions after the death of the Prince Consort in 1861, and gradually he reversed the tradition. The State opening of the Parliament, the Trooping of the Colour, the celebration of the Queen's Birthday, the launching of ships, the visits to industrial towns, the inspection of the armed forces, the patronage of worthy causes, the celebration of coronations and jubilees, and generally the Queen's social functions, are all part of the process of government on whose performance the Queen needs advice. Even her private life may be a matter of public importance, as Edward VIII showed. In the matter of that king's proposed marriage to the present Duchess of Windsor the Prime Minister's advice was decisive.

The existence of the monarchy generally enables us to avoid the problem which republics have always to face, that there are times when a party politician has to speak for the nation. If the national sentiment has to be expressed it is usually possible to advise the Queen to express it. Coming from her, it carries no political implications when, if it came from one who was or had been a party politician, an element of controversy could not be kept out. Even so, there are times when functions of this kind have to be exercised by the Prime Minister. One example will suffice. In 1951 the University of Glasgow celebrated its five hundredth anniversary. At a dinner given by the University to the representatives of other universities, Commonwealth and foreign, the Prime Minister, Mr Attlee, was the principal speaker. His speech was carefully phrased to avoid partisanship; and when he left early to catch the night mail to London, the whole audience, among whom probably four-fifths of those who had votes in the United Kingdom would quite cheerfully have voted him out of office, spontaneously rose to its feet. He was not merely a Labour Prime Minister: he was Prime Minister, the representative of the people of Britain. In the House of Commons, too, he is sometimes the representative of Britain when he rises to move a vote of congratulations or condolence.

The Prime Minister is essentially a party leader. Formally his position may differ according to his party. A Conservative Prime Minister is elected by and technically removable by a body consisting of the Parliamentary Party (all the Conservative Lords and Members), the adopted candidates, and the National Union of Conservative Associations: but the election is always unanimous and a motion to remove him from office would be evidence of such a serious division of opinion in the party that it would be moved only in the most extreme case. He is virtually in control of the Conservative Central Office, the central organization of the party. A Labour Prime Minister has, formally, no such strong position. He is merely leader of the Parliamentary Labour Party and *ex officio* a member of the National Executive Committee of the Labour Party. The difference is not very great in practice, for the essential function of a Prime Minister is to keep his party behind him. Even a Conservative Prime Minister, like Baldwin, may have to battle with dissident elements, while a Labour Prime Minister has always a left wing which wants to go somewhere more quickly, though it is not always sure where it wants to go. What the party has to do is to win the next general election, and on this subject opinions may differ. What is certain is that if the party splits it will lose the election. In the opinion of Disraeli, Peel's greatest defect was that he split his party in 1846, and so condemned it to long years of opposition. Gladstone split the Liberal Party in 1885 and (though he became Prime Minister again in 1892) the Liberals never had real power again until 1906. Lloyd George split the Liberal Party in 1916 and it never again obtained office. Ramsay MacDonald in 1931 condemned the Labour Party to fifteen years of opposition. The management of the party majority, both in Parliament and in the country, is therefore a fundamental task, to which he must direct much of his energy.

The problem in Parliament is different from the problem outside. In Parliament are a few hundred party members, of whom a hundred are members of the Government. Being politicians, they think highly of themselves, and, being peers and members, they have some reason for doing so. The new member, who roared like a lion in his constituency, tends to feel isolated in Parliament. Nobody bothers about him unless he makes himself a nuisance: he is expected to vote frequently and to speak rarely. The Government Whips look after him, and the Prime Minister controls the Whips. A Prime Minister like Churchill, who can joke with anybody, has a great advantage over a Prime Minister like Neville Chamberlain, who had consciously to unbend. Outside Parliament, the Prime Minister is less a person than a personality. Unless members of the Royal Family are present he is top of the bill. He is in fact much like a film star though, not being employed by a profit-making company, he has no publicity manager to see that he hits the headlines. Even so, he must if possible build himself a reputation. His hair style, his pipe, his cigar, even his umbrella or his bald head, may help. On the other hand, the management of the party cannot be carried out by theatrical gestures. It involves careful attention to the shifts of opinion, an almost intuitive understanding of the ordinary man's way of thought, a capacity to tread warily through the web of intrigue which ambitious politicians weave about them, and in short a truly remarkable capacity for judgement. Of all recent Prime Ministers, Baldwin was perhaps the most successful in this sphere because he was wily as a party manager and yet appeared in public as the simple rustic: he combined the wisdom of the serpent with the innocence of the dove.

Next, the Prime Minister is chairman of the Cabinet. He must pick a team and keep it as a team. A team of politicians is probably the most difficult to handle because, though each of them knows that his political future depends on the success of the team, there will usually be a few who are anxious to become captain. It is never very easy to draw the line between personal ambition and anxiety for the public weal. Some would place Joseph Chamberlain among the political prophets; others would regard him as an ambitious politician who twice took the wrong turning. Whatever the explanation may be, he was an uncomfortable colleague even for a Gladstone or a Balfour. His contemporary, Sir William Harcourt, was almost as difficult. More recently there have been other examples – Lloyd George, Churchill (in Baldwin's Government), Cripps (before the War) and Aneurin Bevan. Even when the Cabinet contains no obstreperous member, it is not easy to secure rapid agreement on a wide variety of controversial issues. Public opinion helps, but it never quite knows where it is going, and Cabinets must frequently take unpopular decisions because the consequences of any other decisions would be even more unpopular.

Examples occur almost weekly. Frequently the choice lies between bad alternatives, the one preferred by one section of the Cabinet, the other by the other section. The Prime Minister may try to force his own opinion on the Cabinet, as Gladstone almost always did, and thereby run the risk of splitting the party. He may seek to persuade a minority or convince a majority. He may try to temporize, as Balfour had to do over Tariff Reform. He may compromise, like Aberdeen in 1856 – though that is not a happy precedent, for the compromise led to the Crimean War which history now pronounces to be foolish. He may feel it necessary to give way to the majority even when he does not agree. The management of the Cabinet is certainly the Prime Minister's most difficult function, because it compels him to take difficult decisions not only on the substance but also on the tactics.

The Prime Minister is not, however, concerned only with Cabinet questions. He must keep an eye on what goes on in the Departments. Sir Robert Peel, who is regarded by many as the model Prime Minister in this respect – since he split his party in 1846 he can hardly be regarded as the model in all respects – knew everything of importance that was under discussion by his Ministers and intervened when he considered it necessary. Such close attention is no longer possible now that the functions of government have expanded so widely, but since any Ministerial decision may cause political controversy, the Prime Minister must at least keep one ear open. Usually, though, he exercises supervision through the eagerness of Ministers to consult him. His success depends upon his ability to give sound advice almost on the spur of the moment. With the Foreign Secretary he is in the closest contact, for foreign affairs are always on the agenda. His physical proximity to the Chancellor of the Exchequer – who lives next door in 11 Downing Street – permits of regular consultation. For the rest, his door must ever be open, his mind clear and his judgement rapid and efficient. If he is intellectually lazy like Baldwin or difficult of approach like MacDonald, he cannot exercise these functions properly.

Next, there is the function of managing the House of Commons. This is not quite the same as that of managing the party majority, for the House has a life and a tradition of its own. What is more, the relationship with the party is established in private, whereas the House has to be managed in public. The specific function of arranging the business of the House is nowadays generally left to another Minister, perhaps the Lord Privy Seal or the Lord President of the Council, who is given appointment as Leader of the House: but this delegation cannot deprive the Prime Minister of his function as leader of the Government. The problem is not that the Government runs the risk of defeat – for unless the party breaks up, or has no majority, or has a very small majority, the Government cannot be defeated – but that it runs the risk of being worsted in the argument. The House is 'the finest platform in Europe', the only debating society in Britain whose debates are read, or at least glanced at, by millions. If a Government is to keep its majority in the country, it must consistently make a good case. It may win at every division but lose the next election. Moreover, the House is a temperamental body: it reacts forcibly to any neglect and soon causes its displeasure to be known. The Prime Minister ought therefore to be what is called 'a good House of Commons man', a man who observes its traditions and knows how to handle it, a man like Baldwin or Churchill.

This by no means exhausts the list of functions. The Prime Minister advises the appointment of bishops in consultation with the Archbishop of Canterbury, the superior judges in consultation with the Lord Chancellor, Permanent Secretaries in consultation with the Permanent Secretary to the Treasury, etc. He advises the conferment of honours in the Prime Minister's list, those conferred 'for political and public purposes'. Continually, too, there is the problem of his own Ministry. Its composition is not fixed when he first compiles the list. Some holders of offices will succeed and some will fail; some would do better in different offices; from time to time there will be vacancies due to death or resignation. The recent tendency, begun by Churchill and continued by Attlee, has been to make changes more frequently.

Though it has been necessary to list those functions under different headings, they nearly all hang together. All roads in the Constitution lead to the Prime Minister. From the Prime Minister lead the roads to the Queen, Parliament, the Ministries, the other members of the Commonwealth, even the Church of England and the Courts of Law. Among his colleagues he is said to be *primus inter pares*, first among equals, but it is doubtful if this has been true at any time since Gladstone became Prime Minister in 1868. Harcourt said that he was a moon among lesser stars, but the lesser stars – as they seem to the naked eye – have no connexion with the moon: and the Prime Minister is much more like the sun among the planets.

It is obvious that no Prime Minister will exercise all his functions equally well, for they demand qualities too varied in type. Oddly enough, though, there are very few failures, for success in the House of Commons is usually a guarantee of success as Prime Minister. The great exception of the present century, Ramsay MacDonald, had made his mark on the platform, not in Parliament, and he had had no previous Ministerial experience before he became Prime Minister in 1924. He never learned to handle either the House or his colleagues. On the other hand, Baldwin, an obscure back-bencher until Bonar Law made him Chancellor of the Exchequer in 1922, was superb as a tactician, though too careless to control his team. Neville Chamberlain had little opportunity to show his skill, for he became involved in the preliminaries of the war and foreign affairs were not his *métier*. War administration requires qualities of a very different type, those of a Lloyd George or a Churchill.

LAW AND OPINION

ONE of the peculiarities of English history is that though the courts became subject to the authority of Parliament they retained a great prestige. Parliament and the courts, the statute law and the common law, have so to speak been in alliance, an alliance between equals, in spite of the fact that Parliament could override the courts and the statute law supersede the common law. The high prestige of the judges is peculiar to countries which follow the English tradition.

The explanation is, no doubt, that both Parliament and the courts took their authority from the King and then formed an alliance against the King. The word 'court' has gradually acquired a specialist meaning, a meeting in which the Queen's justices administer law in the Queen's name. There are, however, relics of a wider meaning, as when debutantes are 'presented at court' or an ambassador is accredited to 'the Court at St James'. The King held court when he appeared in public, discussed matters with his courtiers, heard petitions, and issued orders on them, decided disputes between persons subject to his jurisdiction, received ambassadors from foreign sovereigns, received homage from those who had succeeded as his tenants in chief, knighted the sons of great lords, and so on. These functions were gradually differentiated. Some functions are exercised by the High Court of Parliament, some by Her Majesty's Courts of Justice, and some by the Queen herself when she holds a court. The High Court of Parliament became the greatest of the courts; the Queen's orders in Parliament – called Acts of Parliament – are binding upon Her Majesty's judges and will be enforced by them in her Courts of Justice.

In medieval England, though, Acts of Parliament were few. The law of England was developed not in Parliament but in the King's other courts, the courts of justice. The supremacy which the King's courts obtained over the other feudal courts and over the local courts of Anglo-Saxon England created a single, coherent system of law, the common law of England. Whereas other countries had a mass of local customs which had eventually to be superseded by a code of laws, England had a single system, applied by the King's courts in the King's name. This common law obtained high authority because it emanated from the King and was applied by his justices in his name. It contained, too, principles to which politicians could appeal against the King himself. Two characteristics of the English Revolutions are remarkable. One is the extent to which constitutional battles were fought in the courts, in leading cases which still find an honoured place in our books. The other is the way in which lawyer-politicians dominated the debates in Parliament and quoted precedents at enormous length. The lead was given by Coke after his dismissal from the office of Chief Justice, for he believed that liberty was to be secured by following the principles derived from the precedents to be found in the learning of the common law which he 'shovelled up in vast disorderly heaps'. He had with him another great lawyer, John Selden, almost equally learned in the 'black-letter' law books. The lawyers were less prominent after the Restoration and at the Revolution of 1688, for the period of domination by the great landowners was beginning. The attempts made to 'legitimate' the accession of William and Mary were, however, a remarkable tribute to the power of the common law.

The emphasis of this common law of the Constitution was placed not on theoretical principles of political obligation but on practical principles of legal administration. The conflict between Prerogative and Parliament was, in large measure, a conflict over prerogative courts, the right of taxation, the suspension of and dispensing from the laws, arbitrary arrest, trial by jury, habeas corpus. Though the courts could be overruled by Parliament, they could not be overruled outside Parliament. It was their duty to see that the law was observed, even against the King's officers. A public opinion developed after the Restoration, and the subjects debated in the Commons were also debated in the coffee-houses. This public opinion was concerned not so much with constitutional rights as with constitutional wrongs and constitutional remedies. The common law was concerned with the protection of liberties by granting constitutional remedies; and the function of Parliament was not to destroy the common law but to fulfil it by removing, for instance, qualifications and restrictions on the writ of habeas corpus.

This remarkable alliance between Parliament and the courts, statute law and common law, political opinion and popular opinion, continued in the eighteenth century. John Wilkes became a national hero not because he was cast in a heroic mould but because two legal questions were fought over him: whether a Secretary of State could issue a 'general warrant' for the arrest or the seizure of the papers of a person unnamed, and whether the House of Commons could by a resolution disqualify a person from election to the House. These problems were thought worthy of the attention of the greatest statesman of the age, William Pitt, Earl of Chatham. What is more, the American Revolution was fought over legal issues: whether the Parliament of Great Britain could tax the American colonies without their consent. Here not only William Pitt but also the greatest publicist of the period, Edmund Burke, thought it necessary to collect the precedents and discuss the legal issues as part of the wider issues of personal and political liberty.

The French Revolution caused reaction in a Britain which was rapidly becoming industrialized. The land-owning class feared the ideas of liberty and equality which were spreading among the rapidly growing urban working class, and the hardly less dangerous – in an economic sense – industrial middle class. The flag of liberty secured an unlikely standard-bearer in Charles James Fox. He, it is true, knew little of the law, and perhaps cared less, but necessarily the Foxite Whigs emphasized the ancient liberties which were believed to have been secured by the Revolution of 1688. Fox's name was attached to the Libel Act of 1792 which reverted to the old rule – exhibited in the *Case of the Seven Bishops* but denied by Lord Mansfield as

Chief Justice – that in a case of seditious libel the jury was to bring in a verdict of guilty or not guilty and not merely to decide whether there was proof of publication. This Act enabled juries to adopt what seemed to them to be a commonsense view of sedition instead of the legalistic and oppressive view which the judges would probably have adopted. Notwithstanding the enactment of oppressive legislation in the notorious 'Six Acts' of 1817, the reluctance of juries to convict persons who seemed to them merely to have expressed opinions not favoured by unrepresentative Governments re-established the freedom and tolerance which had been characteristic of Britain during most of the eighteenth century.

This history shows how deeply the principles of constitutional law had bitten into public opinion which broadened as larger sections of the people became wealthy and literate in the development of the Industrial Revolution. Even the necessary reform of the police, which Peel introduced in 1829, was resisted as an attack on liberty, with the consequence that the policeman became not an instrument of a despotic Government, but the 'Bobby' standing at the street corner anxious to help anybody in trouble. The popular prejudices exhibited not only in the leading articles and the debates in Parliament, but also in the saloon bar and the tap-room, are founded upon a long tradition of opposition to interference with individual liberty. 'It ain't right' and 'they didn't oughter do it' are relics of ancient constitutional conflicts. Coke and Selden, Pym and Hampden, Pitt and Burke, Fox and the defendants of oppressive litigation, have written their opinions into popular ideas.

This is important in two respects. First, it makes Parliament a rapid and efficient instrument for protection against interference with individual liberty. The House of Commons is at its best when individual grievances of some constitutional importance are raised, even by persons of as little merit as John Wilkes. Secondly, the courts enjoy public esteem in the protection of liberty. It protects them against political interference and enables them to exercise their functions 'freely and fairly, without favour and without fear'.

THE INDEPENDENCE OF THE JUDICIARY

In the absence of a favourable public opinion, no consti-
tional formulae could protect the independence of the
judiciary. The authority of Parliament is wide enough to
destroy it at a blow. Nevertheless, the formulae have been
devised. A judge of a superior court is appointed either by
the Lord Chancellor or by the Prime Minister in consultation with the Lord Chancellor. Until recently political
considerations were not excluded. It can probably be said
that not more than three cases of political influence have
occurred in the past fifty years. Once appointed, though, the
judge is utterly independent. He holds his office not 'at the
pleasure of the Crown', like most royal officers, but 'during
good behaviour'. Possibly there is a legal remedy against a
judge who misuses his office: but since the question has
never arisen in practice, the law is doubtful. The political
remedy is a resolution by both Houses of Parliament, and
this remedy has never been used since it was laid down in
the Act of Settlement in 1701.

The judge's salary, too, is not voted annually like the
salaries of most royal officers. It is 'charged on the Consoli-
dated Fund' like the Queen's Civil List. Nor may a judge
be criticized in Parliament except on a substantive motion.
It follows that, though Parliament can criticize judicial
administration if it is seriously wrong, it cannot criticize
individual judges unless there is clear evidence of mis-
behaviour. The very idea of political interference in judicial
administration is anathema.

These constitutional devices do not equally protect
judicial administration at lower levels, and yet judges and
magistrates in inferior courts are equally independent. One
reason, which applies to all professional judges, is that they
are chosen from a profession which has made independence
its motto. Judges are not civil servants belonging to the
judicial branch of the public service. They are chosen from
the Bar, which has a long tradition of professional independence. The lawyers claim that they belong to the oldest

profession but one in the world. Possibly the claim is not justified, for the priests came before the lawyers. It can be said, though, that in England the Bar is the oldest organized profession. Whereas in most other countries the lawyers were university graduates, in England the pleaders at the King's court at Westminster formed their own organization and controlled the admission of their own members. The Inns of Court began as mere unofficial organizations for communal living, like the colleges of Oxford and Cambridge. They gradually established a monopoly for the admission of 'utter barristers', barristers who plead outside the Bar. The sergeants-at-law, who pleaded within the Bar, received a patent from the Crown, but formed their own Inn. The judges of the supreme courts were appointed from among the sergeants and remained as members of Sergeants' Inn. When the order of sergeants began to disappear the judges were selected from among the King's counsel, barristers who received patents of precedence from the Crown which required them to advise the Crown if need be. As such, they were entitled to plead within the bar, but they remained members of their own Inns. The result is that the judges now remain in the Inns which they entered as students, and by which they were called to the Bar. The fraternity of the Bar is very real, and the barrister who 'submits with all respect' in court need not be so respectful outside the court. There is a professional opinion which carries weight. That opinion, too, strongly favours judicial independence. A subservient judge, a judge who bowed to political pressure or public opinion, would be condemned by his fellows in his own Inn. Thus judicial independence is secured by constitutional devices, strengthened by professional opinion, and founded on public opinion.

Nor have the judges been backward in protecting themselves. For the last 250 years, at least, the judges have echoed Lord Coke's retort to James I, that 'he would do what it was meet a judge should do'. They have held that no judge is liable for words spoken in the course of judicial administration unless he was acting outside his jurisdiction – and the exception cannot apply to a superior judge because he has unlimited jurisdiction. They have, too, developed the offence of contempt of court, which protects the judges from allegations of partiality or incompetence.

The independence of the judiciary is thus secured by a network of constitutional devices and by the force of professional and public opinion. No allegation of partiality or corruption or political influence is ever made against British judges. They share the characteristic of the ordinary Englishman. They are not only independent but truculently independent. Anybody who has the law on his side has the judges on his side. Whatever defects there may be in the law, the citizen is assured that it will be administered freely and fairly, without favour and without fear.

FUNCTIONS OF THE JUDICIARY

Exactly what fields of administration ought to be exercised by courts is a matter on which differences of opinion are possible. The courts have three characteristics. They are independent and impartial; they are staffed (except at petty sessions) by persons trained in the law who have, generally, acquired a wide knowledge of humanity but have no technical knowledge; and they have a highly efficient system for establishing facts which is, however, dilatory and expensive. Clearly they should exercise ordinary civil and criminal jurisdiction, but there are difficulties at the margin. A difference of opinion between the State and John Doe is not necessarily a problem for settlement by an impartial arbitrator. For instance, if a local authority wishes to acquire Blackacre compulsorily in order to establish a children's home, the owner may well object; he bought Blackacre in order to live there peaceably to the end of his days; and, even though he is paid a good price, it is a serious inconvenience to him to have to go house-hunting. This kind of problem can of course be settled by a court. The local authority can brief counsel to explain the public advantages of taking Blackacre rather than some other land; John Doe can brief counsel to explain the inconvenience which he will suffer. This is, however, a dilatory

and expensive way of answering a simple question, whether
the needs of the community in this particular case are
sufficiently great to justify the inconvenience to John Doe.
That question is more easily answered by an inspector of
the Ministry of Local Government than by a court, and the
only expense involved is the travelling allowance of the
inspector. Again, the assessment of John Doe's compensation
can be undertaken by a court, each side calling expert
evidence about values. It is, however, easier and cheaper to
give the job to an independent valuer. Nor is this the only
type of case. The question whether a person is unemployed
and 'genuinely seeking work' is capable of being decided by
a court, and it is important to the person concerned because
it will decide whether he is entitled to insurance benefit.
Nevertheless, if he has to take the official to court he will
never get justice; and if the official has to take the insured
person to court that person may never get benefit. There
are many cases of this character, in which delay and expense
are important. As a learned judge once remarked: 'The
courts are open to everyone, like the Ritz Hotel'.

As the State has intervened more and more in social and
economic affairs in recent years, there have been many
arguments over the boundaries of jurisdiction. The lawyers
tend to assume that the officials, in their anxiety to extend
their own powers, have been encroaching on the functions
of the courts. *Bureaucracy Triumphant* and *The New Despotism*
were the titles of two of the books published around 1930.
The officials, on the other hand, tend to think that the
lawyers are obstructive and antagonistic to essential
reforms. Since the civil service is a silent service, it wrote no
books and its observations, if any, will have been kept in
confidential files. Probably, though, it was noted that most
of those who objected to the distribution of the jurisdiction
objected equally to the nature of the legislation, and that,
whereas more work for officials merely meant more officials,
more work for lawyers meant more fees.

The issue has been confused by the belief that there is a
group of easily definable functions which may be classed as
'judicial' and marked off from another group which may be

classed as 'executive' or 'administrative'. The third group of functions, not at present relevant, but on which the civil service is also said to have encroached, is classed as 'legislative'. This threefold division of powers, which is to be found in Aristotle, was referred to by John Locke, the defender of the Glorious Revolution, and elaborated into a principle by Montesquieu in his study of the English Constitution. Montesquieu did not in fact quite produce the modern classification, which seems to be due to Madison in *The Federalist*, the document designed to defend the draft Constitution of the United States of America. Its plausibility in Britain derives from the fact that there really are three different central authorities in London, the Parliament sitting at Westminster, the Government Departments nearby in Whitehall, and the Royal Courts of Justice in the Strand. Nor is this geographical division purely an accident of history, because all three contribute to our system of government. We can say off-hand that the criminal law should be made by our representatives at Westminster and nowhere else, that a criminal ought to be tried with due formality and the utmost care by an independent and impartial judge like the judges in the Strand, and that if he is found guilty and condemned to imprisonment he should be placed in a prison controlled from Whitehall.

When we try to define 'executive' and 'judicial', however, we find that it cannot be done. The fact that there is an empirical division between Whitehall and the Strand does not necessarily imply that there is a logical division. The life of the law of the Constitution has been not logic but experience. Sometimes it is not even experience nor yet expediency, but just history. The administration of insolvent estates, the care of wards in Chancery, the control of trusts, might have been allocated either to the Strand or Whitehall. The fact is that there is no class of acts called 'judicial' nor a class of acts called 'executive'. As a result of criticisms by the lawyers in the twenties the Lord Chancellor set up a Committee on Ministers' Powers, which reported in 1932. It did its best to define a 'judicial' function but completely failed because it defined in terms of procedure. Even then it produced a class of functions called 'quasi-judicial'. To say that a function is judicial when a judicial procedure is used is to say that an elephant is an elephant if she gives birth to an elephant. The question which we have to ask is whether a function should be given to Whitehall, where an administrative process will be used, or to the Strand, where a judicial process will be used. Even this is not an exact formulation, because it assumes that 'administrative process' and 'judicial process' can be defined.

No argument is needed to assert that the management of the Royal Navy should be allocated to Whitehall and the trial of persons accused of crime to the Strand. The question whether an order to repair defective drains should be issued by a sanitary inspector or a justice of the peace is not so easily decided. In this borderland of administration are many of the functions of the modern State. It will be found that there are both advantages and disadvantages in allocating a function either to an official or to a court. The official is more experienced in this particular field, has a better knowledge of the consequences of default (e.g. in respect of defective drains), and has a more rapid and cheaper procedure. On the other hand the judge is independent, has no axe to grind, is more cautious in jumping to conclusions, has greater experience in the weighing of evidence, and usually pays more attention to the interest of the citizen. In such conditions all that one can do is to weigh the advantages against the disadvantages.

What is interesting is the attitude which creates the controversy, the notion that even the State must be careful of private rights, the belief that the official may be oppressive or impatient while the judge will be cautious and impartial. Though the Committee on Ministers' Powers did not succeed in segregating a judicial function from an administrative function, it did succeed in devising methods to prevent executive excesses. Its mere existence bore witness to the care which English law takes of the interests of the citizen.

What is more, the courts have developed a procedure for keeping administrative authorities under control. If Parliament confers a power upon an official the courts must recognize that power, but they may insist that he exercise it in such a way as not to prejudice the citizen. If Parliament has prescribed the procedure, the courts must recognize the validity of that procedure, but they may see that it operates freely and without bias. Above all the courts will ensure that no official exceeds his powers. The fact that he acted *bona fide* and in the public interest, or that he was acting under superior orders and in the name of the Queen, is not a defence. The Crown and its officials have vast powers, but those powers are closely defined by law. Even in time of emergency, though there are special powers, there are limits beyond which the Queen's Government may not venture without express parliamentary authority. On the war memorial in Lincoln's Inn is inscribed the maxim, 'Inter arma silent leges'. That maxim is bad law. It comes from *The Case of Shipmoney*, where the decision of the majority was declared by Parliament to be wrong. In time of war the Queen has wider powers, but the laws are not silent; they still determine what her powers are, and any of her subjects can take legal proceedings if they are exceeded.

The writ of habeas corpus keeps rising in English history because it was and still is the ultimate legal remedy to protect the liberty of the subject. It is significant of English liberty that a highly technical remedy of this kind should become the subject of political agitation. The right to freedom of the person is useless if there is no court to enforce it or no remedy which the court can use. There are, however, other remedies of the same kind, more frequently needed in modern times. The writ of prohibition enables the court to issue an order upon an inferior 'court' to restrain it from exceeding its jurisdiction, and the writ of certiorari to quash a decision which has been taken without jurisdiction. The writ of mandamus enables the court to order an official, upon whom a duty had been imposed, to carry out that duty, while the writ of quo warranto could be used to compel an official to prove that he held his office. These writs have been superseded by other remedies, more rapid, cheaper and more effective, but their essential principles remain in the law. An official is required by law to do his duty, not to exceed his powers, and to exercise his functions in a fair and impartial manner.

What is more, if an official commits a wrong in the course of his duties he is liable as a private citizen and can be sued in the courts. This admirable principle was not as effective in practice as it would seem at first blush. The Queen could not be sued in her own courts, though a procedure (petition of right) was devised for breaches of contract. To some extent her mantle covered all central officials, because they were her servants. Hence, though the negligence of a private lorry driver, in the course of his duty, makes his employer liable, the negligence of a military lorry driver could not make his employer liable because the Queen was his employer. This problem was not a very serious one in practice, because usually the Crown paid the damages. Nevertheless, there was no legal right to such payment, and so the law was altered in 1947.

GOVERNMENT ACCORDING TO LAW

This discussion has brought us round a circle, for we are back where we began, with Magna Carta and the Rule of Law. The official shares the healthy respect of the citizen for the law. His powers – or the powers of the Queen or the Minister which he exercises – are closely circumscribed by law. British legislation is in sharp contrast with the legislation of countries which have not followed the British tradition. It is not merely empowering legislation, conferring on the Queen or the Minister or the official a general power to solve a particular social or economic problem. It goes into vast detail, specifying what the Queen or the Minister or the official may do, how it may be done, and what remedies are available to those who suffer from administrative action. It is true that other details are left to be laid down by the Minister in statutory instruments, but the power of issuing such instruments is itself closely circumscribed: there is nowhere in the law a general power of *règlementation* - a word for the making of general rules in execution of the laws which has to be put into French because the idea itself does not exist in Britain.

This detailed regulation by law assumes the right and the duty of the courts to intervene wherever it is alleged that the official has exceeded or misused the powers conferred upon him, or upon the Queen or the Minister in whose name he acts. The courts assume this power as a matter of course, and they have invented and developed the forms of procedure necessary for the purpose. The constitutional conflicts of the seventeenth century were carried on in the courts as well as in Parliament and accustomed the courts to the discussion of the highest matters of State. The Revolution established their independence and enabled the tradition of 'tough old Coke' to be carried on by his successors. The Queen is treated with all the respect which her high office warrants: but the legal entity, the Crown, is always regarded with a certain suspicion. The official as such is not a person apart: he is merely a citizen endowed with special powers which he is expected to exercise with rigid honesty and efficiency. The defence of the public interest is not a defence, for the public interest is the sum total of private interests, and it is not in the public interest that injustice be committed. The Government has the legal power to govern, but it must govern according to law.

Further Reading

*

THE British Constitution has been the subject of a larger literature than any Constitution in the world. Its history may be studied in *The Constitutional History of Mediaeval England* by J. E. A. Jolliffe, and *The Constitutional History of Modern Britain* by D. L. Keir (both published by A. & C. Black). The best approach to the law is through *The Law of the Constitution* by A. V. Dicey, 6th ed. by E. C. S. Wade (Longmans, Green & Co. Ltd), with which should be contrasted *The Law and the Constitution*, 5th ed., by Sir Ivor Jennings (University of London Press, Ltd). An introduction to the English political theorists may be obtained from three volumes in the Home University Library on *Political Thought in England*.

The classical exposition of the British Constitution is that of Walter Bagehot, of which there are many editions. The most accessible is that in the World's Classics (Oxford University Press), with an introduction by Lord Balfour. The present author's views may be studied in *The British Constitution* (Cambridge University Press, 5th ed.), which is based mainly on his larger works, *Cabinet Government* (Cambridge University Press, 3rd ed.) and *Parliament* (Cambridge University Press, 2nd ed.). A different approach is possible through *Parliamentary Government in England* by H. J. Laski (Allen & Unwin Ltd) and *Reflections on the Constitution* by the same author (Manchester University Press). The latter is a critique of a book by L. S. Amery, *Thoughts on the Constitution*, which has since appeared in a second edition.

For those who desire a rapid survey of modern constitutional law, the best book is *Constitutional Law* by E. C. S. Wade and G. Godfrey Phillips (Longmans, Green & Co., 4th ed.). The standard work, now sadly out of date, is Sir William Anson's *Law and Custom of the Constitution* (Clarendon Press, 3 vols).

Party politics is dealt with historically by Sir Ivor Jennings, *Party Politics* (Cambridge University Press, 3 vols.) and analytically by R. T. McKenzie, *British Political Parties* (Heinemann, 2nd ed.).

On the legal system reference may be made to *The British Courts of Law* by H. G. Hanbury (Home University Library). The best introduction for lay readers, probably, is *The English Legal Tradition* by H. Levy-Ullman (Macmillan).

Index

*

Adjournment motion, 91
Allegiance, 37
Autonomous authorities, 102–4

Backwoodsmen, 72, 75
Bate's Case, 16
Bentham, Jeremy, 79
Bills, enactment of, 66–7
Bracton, 12
Burke, Edmund, 79, 82, 143, 144

Cabinet, 96–8, 115–31
Cabinet Secretariat, 126–8
Certiorari, 151
Chamberlain, Joseph, 63, 65, 82, 137
Church of England, 17–18, 57–8, 71–2, 139
Civil Service, 104–8, 109–10
Civil War, 15–16, 68–9, 142
Classes, 51–62
Coke, Sir Edward, 10, 12, 15, 16, 142, 144, 146
Collective responsibility, 100–1, 118–25
Common Law, 12, 141, 142
Commons, House of, 68–70, 76–94, 139
Communism, 25–6, 87
Commonwealth, 36–40
Comptroller and Auditor-General, 93, 107
Conservative party, 22, 23, 24, 27, 41, 54, 55, 59, 60, 61, 64, 82–3, 136
Constituencies, 23
Contempt of Court, 147
Corn Laws, 21, 22, 63
Council, Privy, 96–7
Crown, 30–5
Cromwell, Oliver, 17

Defence Committee, 126–7
Delegated legislation, 92–3
Democracy, 20–7, 76–8
Disraeli, Benjamin, 22, 27, 44, 65, 70, 71, 78, 80, 82, 115, 133

Economic interests, 25–6
Equality, 27, 77, 78–80

Financial control, 93–4
Finch, Chief Justice, 12–13
Floating vote, 56–7, 58–60
Fox, Charles James, 143, 144
Franchise, 21–3, 70, 77–8
Free Trade, 54–5
French Revolution, 143

Gas and Water Socialism, 28, 103
Gladstone, W. E., 23, 27, 44, 54, 63, 71, 78, 82, 106, 133, 137, 138, 140

Habeas corpus, 151
Hampden, John, 10, 12, 15, 16, 91, 144
Hansard, 69, 89
Home Rule, 54, 63–4, 73
Honours, 48

India, 38–40
Industrial Revolution, 19, 21, 77–8, 103, 104, 144
Inns of Court, 146

Judges, 145–52

Labour Party, 22, 24, 27, 41, 43, 55, 57, 60, 61, 64, 75, 83, 85, 136

Landed interest, 18–20, 21
Legislation, 93
Liberal Party, 21, 22, 23, 27, 54, 55, 58, 62, 63–4, 82–3
Liberty, 9–13, 23–9, 91–2
Local Government, 101–2
Locke, John, 149
Lords, House of, 71–5

Madison, 149
Magna Carta, 9, 12, 13, 25, 68, 91, 92, 152
Mandamus, 151
Marxism, 79
Middle Class, 14–15, 19, 26, 27, 52–3, 56–65, 69
Mill, J. S., 80
Milton, John, 17
Ministers, 95, 98–101, 108–13, 114–31
Ministers' Powers, Committee on, 149–50
Montesquieu, 149

Nonconformists, 17, 20, 21, 58, 71, 77, 82–3
Non-voters, 58–9

Opposition, 87–92, 111–12, 129–31
Overlords, 117–18, 126

Parliament, dissolution of, 43
meaning of, 66
origin of, 13–14
Queen in, 66–71
sovereignty of, 13–20
Parliament Act, 73–4
Parties, 24, 50–65, 81–90, 136
Patronage, 105
Peel, Sir Robert, 21, 63, 65, 69, 81, 106, 115, 133, 138
Peerage, 72
Pitt, William, 84, 85, 89, 101, 106, 133, 144
Police, 144
Politics, 50–62

Prime Minister, 41–3, 85, 98, 109, 114, 119, 132–40
Prohibition, writ of, 151
Public Accounts Committee, 93–4, 107
Public opinion, 23, 129–31, 142–5
Pym, John, 15, 144

Queen, Commonwealth and, 36–40
Crown and, 30–5
executive function of, 95
functions of, 30–46, 134–5
law and, 12–13
Parliament and, 15–16, 66–70
personal functions of, 40–6
social functions of, 46–9
Questions, 90

Red tape, 92, 107
Reform Act, 21, 69
Religion, 16–18, 57–8
Representation, 76–80
Roman Catholics, 16–17, 34, 57–8
Rule of Law, 9–13, 152–3

Second Chamber, 71–5
Selden, John, 16, 142, 144
Separation of powers, 83–5
Seven Bishops' Case, 143
Shipmoney, Case of, 10, 16, 151
Six Acts, 144
Socialism, 55
Speaker, 14, 67
Statute Law, 141

Tories, 21, 69, 81–2, 98, 99, 100
Trades Unions, 57
Two-party system, 62–5

United States, 36, 84–5

Walpole, Sir Robert, 98, 132
Welfare State, 55–6, 61, 73
Whigs, 21, 69, 81–2, 98, 99, 100
Wilkes, John, 143, 144

Sir Ivor Jennings was born in 1903 and educated at Bristol Grammar School and St Catharine's College, Cambridge, of which he was an Honorary Fellow. He was called to the Bar in 1928, became King's Counsel in 1949, and was a Bencher of Gray's Inn. He was Vice-Chancellor of the University of Ceylon from 1942 to 1955, of the University of Cambridge from 1961–3, and Master of Trinity Hall and Downing Professor of the Laws of England at Cambridge. He held the degrees of Litt.D. of Cambridge, LL.D. of London, and honorary degrees from the Universities of Bristol, Leeds, Southampton, Paris, Ceylon, Hong Kong, and the Queen's University, Belfast.

While in Ceylon he advised the Ceylonese Ministers in the constitutional discussions which led to the Constitution of Ceylon and afterwards was constitutional adviser to the Government of Pakistan. He was knighted for services to Ceylon and made K.B.E. for services to Pakistan. He was a member of the panel of jurists which advised the United Nations about the Constitution of Eritrea and a member of the Malayan Constitutional Commission. He was also constitutional adviser to the Commission which drafted the first Constitution of Nepal. He was chairman of the Social Services Commission of Ceylon, of the Royal Commission on Common Land in England and Wales, and of the Royal University of Malta Commission. He died in 1966.

He wrote a number of books on constitutional matters. They include *The Law and The Constitution, Cabinet Government, Parliament, Party Politics, The British Constitution, The Constitutional Laws of the Commonwealth, The British Commonwealth of Nations, The Commonwealth in Asia, The Constitution of Ceylon, Constitutional Problems in Pakistan,* and *The Approach to Self-Government.*